Miracle Fair

Also by Wisława Szymborska

Miracle Fair

Selected Poems of Wisława Szymborska

translated by Joanna Trzeciak

W. W. Norton & Company | New York London

For information about permission to reproduce selections from this book, write to
Permissions, W. W. Norton & Company, Inc., 500 Fifth Avenue, New York, NY 10110

The text of this book is composed in Bembo
with the display set in Bembo
Book design by Chris Welch
Production manager: Leelo Märjamaa-Reintal

Library of Congress Cataloging-in-Publication Data

Szymborska, Wislawa.
    [Poems. English. Selections]
    Miracle fair: selected poems of Wislawa Szymborska / translated by Joanna
Trzeciak.
        p. cm.
    Includes bibliographical references.
    ISBN: 0-393-04939-6
    1. Szymborska, Wislawa—Translations into English. I. Trzeciak, Joanna. II. Title.

PG7178.Z9 A28 2001
891.8'5173—dc21

                                                                00-051970

ISBN 0-393-32385-4 pbk.

W. W. Norton & Company, Inc., 500 Fifth Avenue, New York, N.Y. 10110
    www.wwnorton.com

W. W. Norton & Company Ltd., Castle House, 75/76 Wells Street, London W1T 3QT

1 2 3 4 5 6 7 8 9 0

to John Huss

Contents

Acknowledgments

The poems in this book have appeared in the following publications

American Poetry Review: "Torture"
Antioch Review: "Some People"
The Atlantic Monthly: "A Word on Statistics," "Openness," "Commemoration"
Beloit Poetry Journal: "The Joy of Writing," "On Death, without Exaggeration"
Boston Book Review: "A Dream," "Clouds"
Boulevard: "People on the Bridge"
Chicago Review: "In Abundance"
DoubleTake: "Starvation Camp at Jasło"
Harper's Magazine: "The End and the Beginning"
Iowa Review: "Psalm," "Parting with a View"
Kenyon Review: "Pursuit," "A Thank-You Note"
The New Republic: "Sky"
The New Yorker: "Some Like Poetry," "I am too close for him . . ."
Paris Review: "Negative"
Ploughshares: "Children of Our Era," "Reality Demands"
Poetry: "A Great Man's House"
River Styx: "Seen from Above," "The Cave"
Ruminator Review: "Drinking Wine," "Thomas Mann," "Surplus," "Birds Returning," "Landscape"
Stand Magazine: "A Note"
Threepenny Review: "The End and the Beginning"
Tin House: "Love at First Sight," "Miracle Fair"
Tikkun: "Still"
The Times Literary Supplement: "In Heraclitus' River"

Tri-Quarterly: "Interview with a Child," "Cat in an Empty Apartment," "The Turn of the Century," "Hatred"

Virginia Quarterly Review: "No Title Required," "One Version of Events," "Rubens' Women," "Under a Certain Little Star," "Water"

* AND discovered this "togetherness," because — NO, just as it happened, of all my bks, these 2 were alone together on my bedstand tonight when these notes written

Foreword by Czeslaw Milosz *

One

Poetry that speaks to the enduring and irreversible coordinates of human fate—love, striving, fear of pain, hope, the fleeting nature of things, and death—leads us to believe that the poet is one of us, and shares in that fate. "We," the subject of such poetry, is determined neither by nation nor by class. But it would not be quite right to claim that its theme is therefore an eternal human nature, for as our consciousness changes, we humans try to confront ultimate things in new and different ways. In Szymborska's poetry the "we" denotes all of us living on this planet now, joined by a common consciousness, a "post-consciousness," post-Copernican, post-Newtonian, post-Darwinian, post-two-World-Wars, post-crimes-and-inventions-of-the-twentieth-century. It is a serious and bold enterprise to venture a diagnosis, that is, to try to say who we are, what we believe in, and what we think.

Two

Szymborska's "I" is an ascetic "I," cleansed not only of the desire to confess, but of any individuating features, and yet it is linked to the "I" of all others who share in the human condition and thus deserve pity and compassion. Although one of her poems bears the title "In Praise of My Sister," the sister appears only as someone who "doesn't write poetry." The poem "Laughter" tells of a conversation with a girl, the poet herself from many years ago, but there is nothing singular in this: it could be a meeting between any two people. Moreover the "he" in "Laughter" goes unnamed; we know nothing about him. Another poem "Clothing," which

*SEE HIRSHFIELD'S Nine Gates, Entering the Mind of Poetry, p. 205[1]
at 1:04AM, 11/3/16.

describes a visit to the doctor's office, begins: "You undress, we undress, you undress"—the use of these three forms of the verb "undress" embodies the essence of Szymborska's poetry: "the singular you," "the plural you," and "the collective we" merge into one. And to cite yet another example, doesn't the poem "A Report from the Hospital" bring us news of what happens to each of "you," to all of "us"?

Three

The consciousness that Szymborska probes is "ours" because we hold it in common, the result of our schooling, the glossy magazines we've read, television, and visits to museums. Now, there may be a villager somewhere in southern India who would not recognize himself in these poems because the frequent references to our past—Homer, Troy, Rome, Lot's wife, the Flood, Mary Stuart, and so forth—would be foreign to him. But in general, on a planet growing ever smaller, increasingly we dine on the same cultural dishes.

Four

Our cultural consciousness is shaped early on in life: We learn from grownups that the Sun does not, in fact, revolve around the Earth, that the Earth is but a speck within an unfathomable whirl of galaxies, that scientists seek to discover the origin of life on earth, that *Homo sapiens* resulted from a long evolutionary process, and that our closest relative is the monkey. The foundation of Szymborska's worldview seems to be biology lessons learned at school—many of her poems find their origins in evolutionary theory itself. Yet she never makes the reductionist turn. On the contrary, to her, man is astonishing, precisely because even though his genealogy is so modest and he is bound up in a fragile body, he nonetheless stands up to nature and creates his own world of art, values, discoveries, and adventures. Man is astonishing because he has "a hand miraculously feathered by a fountain pen" (in (3) "Thomas Mann"), because he summons up the courage to write—the "Revenge of a mortal hand" (in "The Joy of Writ- 127 ing"). The cult of the giant achievements of the human spirit, of the masterpieces of the past preserved in museums or passed on in writing, is counted among the basic ingredients of twentieth-century consciousness. Szymborska cultivates this, mindful that whatever remains is all the more precious for having been torn away from an ever watchful death. Particular to our century is a coming to grips with the fragility of our bodily existence, as treated in one of Szymborska's most moving poems, "Torture": 46

Nothing has changed.
The body is painful,

   because the soul is:

a stranger to itself, evasive,
at one moment sure, the next unsure of its existence,
while the body is and is and is
and has no place to go.

Five

Thus Polish poetry finally has worked its way to existential meditation, leaving behind pure lyric and embarking on discourse, which had always been thought prosaic. At the end of the nineteenth century Adam Asnyk (1838–1897) philosophized in verse in a way that today seems rather unconvincing. During the Polish

Modernist era, Kazimierz Tetmajer (1865–1940) wrote a meditative poem, titled "End of the Century." The poetry of the "Skamander" movement, which flourished in the interwar years, was not distinguished by its intellectual content. A great deal had to happen before the necessary tools could be forged to allow a poet like Szymborska to respond to the clearly perceived need for intelligent discourse on life's cheerless dance. Varied shades of irony and humor became the modern and indispensable seasoning. Szymborska brings joy because she is so sharp, because she derives pleasure out of juggling the props of our common heritage (when she writes about Rubens' women and the Baroque, for example), and because she has such a good sense of the comic. And she takes a conscious risk, performing her magic tricks along the fine line between poem and essay.

She would not have been faithful to the true colors of her times had she preserved their brighter shades. To be frank, hers is a very grim poetry. Because her work is part of world literature, we can hold this diagnosis up to that of others in different languages. A comparison with the despairing vision of Samuel Beckett and Philip Larkin suggests itself. Yet, in contrast to them Szymborska offers a world where one can breathe. Thanks to a thorough relinquishing of subjectivity, "I" and its particular form of personal depression fall by the wayside. They are replaced by a playfulness that gives us, in spite of everything else, a feeling for the enormous diversity and splendor of human existence.

—*translated by Joanna Trzeciak*

Translator's Note

The present volume features a selection of new translations of the poetry of Wisława Szymborska. A substantial number of these poems have never appeared in English translation before. Indeed several had been deemed untranslatable. In the case of poems that have previously been published in my translation in literary periodicals, I have revisited and revised them for this collection.

The poems are laid out in a manner that invites the reader to trace the development of a set of themes coursing through Szymborska's poetry. They are arranged in six thematic clusters, the poet illustrating each theme with a collage of her own making. The title of each of these clusters is a quotation plucked from one of the poems contained therein, emblematic of the spirit and theme of the cluster, and at the same time alive with multiple interpretive possibilities. The choice of themes merely suggests the breadth of Szymborska's poetry, but by no means exhausts it. Within each cluster the poems are ordered chronologically. With the poet's guidance, I have chosen poems that best represent each theme, with no effort to sample all of her collections. Nevertheless, I believe her poetry is well represented here.

I have also provided notes to individual poems with three purposes in mind. Allusions and references contained in the poems are identified and briefly explicated. Translation problems and their solutions are mentioned where appropriate. Finally, some sense of the period in which these poems were written is given. In most cases, dates of publication in book form are provided; however, significant first appearances in periodicals are also noted. Some information in the biographical note and in the notes to individual poems draws from the spirited biography *Pamiątkowe rupiecie, przyjaciele i sny Wisławy Szymborskiej* by Anna Bikont and Joanna Szczęsna (Pruszyński i S-ka: Warsaw, 1997).

The simplicity and economy of Szymborska's poetry pose a challenge to her translators. Though writing in a conversational tone, Szymborska never falls back on idiom; rather, she gently subverts it. Where her language reflects an internal dialogue or dissonance, I have tried to capture that grappling quality rather than smooth it over. In choosing how to render the seemingly untranslatable, I have sought to draw out the possibilities lurking in language rather than compensate through embellishment or augmentation. Szymborska has a penchant for coining new words, and I hope I have preserved the seamlessness with which her coinages and consonantal creatures arise organically from the flow of the original Polish. As for formal considerations, I have tried to remain as faithful to the forms of the original poems as possible, bearing in mind the differences in grammar and poetics between Polish and English. Rhyme schemes were maintained, though slant rhymes were sometimes substituted for straight rhymes.

Because Szymborska draws freely from a wide variety of linguistic registers, choices between alternative translations of individual words were sensitive to frequency of usage. For example, an effort was made to avoid rendering common Polish words by obscure English words. Balanced against this was the desire that connotations be preserved. This prompted some rather difficult translation choices.

These translations are born out of a fascination with Szymborska's poetry that began in my childhood. The list of those to be thanked, no matter how long, could never be exhaustive. I would like most of all to thank Wisława Szymborska for her support with nearly every aspect of this book and for making her collages available to me. The assistance of Michał Rusinek has been indispensable. The unflagging resolve of Szymborska's attorney Marek Bukowski went a long way toward making this volume even remotely possible. Many thanks to Czeslaw Milosz for his enormous generosity of spirit and sustained support. It was an honor and a delight to translate his foreword to this volume.

I started translating Szymborska into English with Marek Lugowski, to whom I feel a debt of gratitude. "Hatred," in the present collection, was co-translated with him. Numerous people have seen and commented on individual poems, caught errors, suggested improvements, and offered encouragement. Most of all, I would like to thank my husband, John Huss, who ruthlessly critiqued my translations from rough draft to final version, and offered suggestions that significantly improved the collection and contributed to its artistic shape. My thanks go to John Alvis, David Davies, Susan Hahn, Marlys and Roger Huss, Jerzy Jarzębski, Michael Latham, Tamara Miller, Kuba Ober, Adrienne and Roger Rosenberg, Samuel Sandler, Tamara Trojanowska, and The TransAtlantic Society. Special thanks go to Mark Strand for his perfect pitch. Jill Bialosky, editor of this collection for W. W. Norton & Company, has been a steady and patient supporter of this volume. My loving thanks go to my parents, Wiesław and Olga, for raising me in a spirit of appreciation for poetry, both Polish and Anglo-American. My brother Sergio was a great source of copied manuscripts and sheer joy. Tadeusz Debski commented extensively and creatively on a larger collection of translations from which the present volume was culled. Jacek Niecko read and commented on the entire manuscript, offering seasoned judgment and undying inspiration.

—*Joanna Trzeciak*
Chicago
25 December 1999

Miracle Fair

. . . for a long time chance had been
toying with them . . .

Commemoration

They made love among hazel shrubs
beneath suns of dew,
gathering in their hair
the forest's residue.

Heart of the swallow
have mercy on them.

They knelt down by the lake,
combed out the earth and leaves,
and fish swam to the water's edge,
a shimmering galaxy.

Heart of the swallow
have mercy on them.

Steam rose from trees reflected
in the rippling waves.
O swallow let this memory
forever be engraved.

O swallow, thorn of clouds,
anchor of the air,
Icarus improved,
Assumption in formal wear,

O swallow, the calligrapher,
timeless second hand,
early ornithogothic,
a crossed eye in the sky,

O swallow, pointed silence,
mourning full of joy,
halo over lovers,
have mercy on them.

Openness

Here we are, naked lovers,
beautiful to each other—and that's enough—
the leaves of our eyelids our only covers,
we're lying amidst deep night.

But they know about us, they know,
the four corners, and the stove nearby us.
Clever shadows also know
the table knows, but keeps quiet.

Our teacups know full well
why the tea is getting cold.
And old Swift can surely tell
that his book's been put on hold.

Even the birds are in the know:
I saw them writing in the sky
brazenly and openly
the very name I call you by.

The trees? Could you explain to me
their unrelenting whispering?
The wind may know, you say to me,
but how, is just a mystery.

A moth surprised us through the blinds,
its wings a fuzzy flutter.
Its silent path—see how it winds
in a stubborn holding pattern.

Maybe it sees where our eyes fail
with an insect's inborn sharpness.
I never sensed, nor could you tell
that our hearts were aglow in the darkness.

Drinking Wine

He looked at me, bestowing beauty,
and I took it for my own.
Happy, I swallowed a star.

I let him invent me
in the image of the reflection
in his eyes. I dance, I dance
in an abundance of sudden wings.

A table is a table, wine is wine
in a wineglass, which is a wineglass
and it stands standing on a table
but I am a phantasm,
a phantasm beyond belief,
a phantasm to the core.

I tell him what he wants to hear—about ants
dying of love
under a dandelion's constellation.
I swear that sprinkled with wine
a white rose will sing.

I laugh, and tilt my head
carefully, as if I were testing
an invention. I dance, I dance
in astounded skin, in the embrace
that creates me.

Eve from a rib, Venus from sea foam,
Minerva from the head of Jove
were much more real.

When he's not looking at me,
I search for my reflection
on the wall. All I see
is a nail on which a painting hung.

I am too close for him . . .

I am too close for him to dream about me.
I'm not flying over him, not fleeing him
under the roots of trees. I am too close.
Not with my voice sings the fish in the net.
Not from my finger rolls the ring.
I am too close. A large house is on fire
without my calling for help. Too close
for a bell dangling from my hair to chime.
Too close for me to enter as a guest
before whom the walls part.
Never again will I die so readily,
so far beyond the flesh, so inadvertently
as once in his dream. I am too close,
too close—I hear the hiss
and see the glittering husk of that word,
as I lie immobilized in his embrace. He sleeps,
more available at this moment
to the ticket lady of a one-lion traveling circus
seen but once in his life
than to me lying beside him.
Now a valley grows for her in him, ochre-leaved,
closed off by a snowy mountain
in the azure air. I am too close
to fall out of the sky for him. My scream
might only awaken him. Poor me,
limited to my own form,
but I was a birch tree, I was a lizard,
I emerged from satins and sundials
my skins shimmering in different colors. I possessed

the grace to disappear from astonished eyes,
and that is the rich man's riches. I am too close,
too close for him to dream about me.
I slip my arm out from under his sleeping head.
It's numb, full of imaginary pins and needles.
And on the head of each, ready to be counted,
dance the fallen angels.

A Dream

My dead-in-battle, my turned-to-ashes, my earth,
taking the shape he has in the photograph:
leaf's shadow on his face, seashell in hand,
he marches unto my dream.

He wanders through darkness frozen since never,
through emptiness opened toward him for always,
through seven times seven times seven silences.

He appears on the inner side of my eyelids,
in the one and only world accessible to him.
His shot-through heart is beating.
A primordial wind gusts from his hair.

A meadow springs up between us.
The sky flies in with clouds and birds,
mountains quietly explode on the horizon
and the river flows down in search of the sea.

One can see so far, so far,
that day and night become simultaneous
and all the seasons are experienced at once.

The moon opens up its four-phased fan,
snowflakes swirl along with butterflies
and fruit falls from a blossoming tree.

We come toward each other. I don't know whether we're in tears
or whether we're smiling. One more step
and we will listen to your seashell,
what a sound, like thousands of orchestras,
what a wedding march.

A Man's Household

He's one of those men who want to do everything by themselves.
You need to love him along with drawers, cabinets, and shelves,
with what's on top of cupboards, or inside or sticking out.
Everything is going to come in handy without a doubt.
Drills, hammers, files, chisels, melting pots, and pliers,
bundles of string, springs and umbrella wires,
squeezed-out tubes, dried-out glue,
jars big and small where something already grew,
an assortment of pebbles, a little anvil, a vise,
an alarm clock that's already been broken twice,
a dead beetle in a soap dish, beside an empty vial,
on which a skull and crossbones have been painted in grand style,
a batten, short and long plugs, buckles, and a gasket,
a Lake Mamry water hen's three feathers in a basket,
a few champagne corks stuck in cement,
two glass slides scorched in the course of an experiment,
a pile of bars, some cardboard boxes, tiles, a gutter spout,
and fitting uses for them all might soon be figured out,
some handles to something, scraps of leather, a blanket torn to
    shreds,
a boyish slingshot, scads of keys, and screws of varied threads . . .
May I throw out a thing or two?—I put this to him dearly,
but in response the man I love just looked at me severely.

A Thank-You Note

I owe a lot
to those I do not love.

Relief in accepting
others care for them more.

Joy that I am not
wolf to their sheep.

Peace be with them
for with them I am free
—love neither gives
nor knows how to take these things.

I don't wait for them
from window to door.
Almost as patient
as a sun dial,
I understand
what love never could.
I forgive
what love never would.

Between rendezvous and letter
no eternity passes,
only a few days or weeks.

Our trips always turn out well:
concerts are enjoyed,
cathedrals toured,
landscapes in focus.

And when seven rivers and mountains
come between us,
they are the rivers and mountains
found on any map.

The credit's theirs
if I live in three dimensions,
in a non-lyrical and non-rhetorical space,
with a real, ever-shifting horizon.

They don't even know
how much they carry in their empty hands.

"I owe them nothing,"
love would have said
on this open topic.

Cat in an Empty Apartment

Dying—you wouldn't do that to a cat.
For what is a cat to do
in an empty apartment?
Climb up the walls?
Brush up against the furniture?
Nothing here seems changed,
and yet something has changed.
Nothing has been moved,
and yet there's more room.
And in the evenings the lamp is not on.

Footsteps on the stairs,
but they're not the same.
Neither is the hand
that puts a fish in the saucer.

Something here isn't starting
at its usual time.
Something here isn't happening
as it should.
Somebody had been here and had been,
and then had suddenly disappeared
and now is stubbornly absent.

All the closets have been peeked in
and all the shelves explored.
Slipping under the carpet and checking came to nothing.
A rule was even broken and all the papers scattered.
What else is there to do?
Sleep and wait.

Just let him come back,
let him show up.
Then he'll find out
you don't do that to a cat.
Going toward him
faking reluctance,
slowly,
on very offended paws.
And no jumping, no purring at first.

Parting with a View

I don't begrudge the spring
for coming back again.
I can't blame it
for doing its duty
the same as every year.

I realize my sorrow
won't halt the greenery.
If a blade wavers,
it's only from the wind.

It doesn't cause me pain,
that clumps of alder above the waters
have something to rustle with again.

I accept
that—as though you were still alive—
the shore of a certain lake
has remained as beautiful as it was.

I don't hold a grudge
against a view for a view
onto a bay dazzled by the sun.

I can even imagine,
that some–not–us
are sitting now
on a toppled birch stump.

I respect their right
to whispers, laughter,
and happy silence.

I even assume
they're bound by love
and that he puts a living arm around her.

Something recently birdly
rustles in the bulrushes.
I sincerely hope
they hear it.

Let them be as they were,
those waves lapping on the shore,
sometimes swift, sometimes lazy,
and obedient not to me.

I ask nothing
of the deep waters below the woods,
emerald,
sapphire,
black.

To one thing I won't agree.
To my return.
The privilege of presence—
that I'll give up.

I've survived you just enough
but only enough,
to reflect from afar.

Love at First Sight

They are sure
that a sudden feeling united them.
Beautiful is such certainty,
but uncertainty more beautiful.

They think, that as they didn't know each other earlier,
nothing ever happened between them.
But what would they say: those streets, stairways, and corridors
where they could have been passing each other for a long time?

I would like to ask them,
don't you remember—
maybe face to face once
in a revolving door?
an "excuse me" in a tight crowd?
a "wrong number" heard over the phone?
—but I know their answer.
No, they don't remember.

They would be quite surprised,
that for a long time
chance had been toying with them.

Not altogether ready
to turn into their fate,
it would draw them together, pull them apart,
cut them off on their path,
and, swallowing a giggle,
leap to the side.

There were signs, signals,
so what they were unreadable.
Maybe three years ago
or last Tuesday
some leaf flew
from arm to arm?
Something got lost and then got picked up.
Who knows whether it wasn't even a ball
in some childhood thicket?

There were doorknobs and doorbells,
where touch lay on touch
beforehand.
Suitcases next to one another in the baggage check.
Maybe one night the same dream,
blurred upon awakening.

Every beginning, after all,
is nothing but a sequel,
and the book of events
is always open in the middle.

Negative

In a grayish sky
a cloud even more gray
with a black outline from the sun.

On the left, that is, on the right,
a white cherry branch with black blossoms.

On your dark face light shadows.
You have sat down at a small table
and laid your grayed hands on it.

You seem like a ghost
trying to summon the living.

(Because I'm still counted among them,
I should appear to him and tap:
good night, that is, good morning,
farewell, that is, hello.
Not begrudging him questions to any answer
if they concern life,
that is, the storm before the calm.)

. . . too much has happened that was not supposed to happen . . .

We knew the world backwards and forwards . . .

We knew the world backwards and forwards—
so small it fit in a handshake,
so easy it could be described in a smile,
as plain as the echoes of old truths in a prayer.

History did not greet us with triumphant fanfare—
it flung dirty sand in our eyes.
Ahead of us were distant roads leading nowhere,
poisoned wells, bitter bread.

The spoils of war is our knowledge of the world—
so large it fits in a handshake,
so hard it could be described in a smile,
as strange as the echoes of old truths in a prayer.

Still

In the sealed cars of freight trains
across the country travel names,
but where are they going to go,
and will they ever get out,
don't ask, can't say, don't know.

Nathan's name bangs his fists on the wall.
Isaac's name sings in a maddened thrall.
Sarah's name cries that the water go first
to Aaron's name which is dying of thirst.

Do not jump off the train, David's name.
You're the name that has been condemned,
given to no one without a home,
too heavy to bear in this land.

To the son goes a Slavic name as it should,
for here they count the hairs on your head,
for here they divide the bad from the good
based on a name or the shape of an eyelid.

Do not jump off the train. Lech is the name he will have.
Do not jump off the train. There's still time to hold back.
Do not jump. The night spreads like a laugh
mocking the clatter of wheel upon track.

A cloud made of people passed over the land.
From a large cloud a small rain, a sole tear was shed,
a small rain, a sole tear, a season of lack.
Into a forest of black veer the tracks.

That's so that's so, go the wheels.
These woods have no clearing.
That's so that's so.
A cargo of cries disappearing.
That's so that's so.
Awakened in deep night on hearing
that's so that's so,
the clatter of silence on silence.

Starvation Camp at Jasło

Write this down. Write it. In ordinary ink
on ordinary paper: they were given no food,
all died of hunger. *All. How many?*
It's a large meadow. How much grass
was there per person? Write it down: I don't know.
History rounds off skeletons to the nearest zero.
A thousand and one is still a thousand.
As if that one weren't there at all:
an imaginary embryo, empty cradle,
a primer opened for no one,
air that laughs and screams and grows,
stairs for the void running down to the garden,
nobody's place in the ranks.

This is the meadow where it became flesh.
But the meadow is silent as a bribed witness.
In the sunlight. Green. Over there is a forest
for chewing wood, for drinking from under bark—
a daily helping of landscape,
until one goes blind. Up there is a bird,
that moved across lips as a shadow
of its nutritious wings. Jaws opened,
teeth would chomp.
At night a sickle would flash in the sky,
reaping dreamt-up grain for dreamt-up loaves.
Hands of blackened icons would fly in,
bearing empty goblets.

On a spit of barbed wire
a man was swaying.
They were singing with soil in their mouths. *A lovely song*
about the way war hits you right in the heart.
Write about the silence here.
Yes.

Psalm

How leaky are the borders of man-made states!
How many clouds float over them scot-free,
how much desert sand sifts from country to country,
how many mountain pebbles roll onto foreign turf
in provocative leaps!

Need I cite each and every bird as it flies,
or alights, as now, on the lowered gate?
Even if it be a sparrow—its tail is abroad,
though its beak is still home. As if that weren't enough—it keeps
    fidgeting!

Out of countless insects I will single out the ant,
who, between the guard's left and right boots,
feels unobliged to answer questions of origin and destination.

If only this whole mess could be seen at once in detail
on every continent!
Isn't that a privet on the opposite bank
smuggling its hundred-thousandth leaf across the river?
Who else but the squid, brazenly long-armed,
would violate the sacred territorial waters?

How can we speak of any semblance of order
when we can't rearrange the stars
to know which one shines for whom?

Not to mention the reprehensible spreading of fog!
Or the dusting of the steppe over its entire range
as though it weren't split in two!
Or voices carried over accommodating air waves:
summoning squeals and suggestive gurgles!

Only what's human can be truly alien.
The rest is mixed forest, undermining moles, and wind.

The Turn of the Century

It was supposed to be better than the rest, our twentieth century.
But it won't have time to prove it.
Its years are numbered,
its step unsteady,
its breath short.

Already too much has happened
that was not supposed to happen,
and what was to come
has yet to come.

Spring was to be on its way,
and happiness, among other things.

Fear was to leave the mountains and valleys.
The truth was supposed to finish before the lie.

Certain misfortunes
were never to happen again
such as war and hunger and so forth.

The defenselessness of the defenseless
was going to be respected.
Same for trust and the like.

Whoever wanted to enjoy the world
faces an impossible task.

Stupidity is not funny.
Wisdom is not cheerful.

Hope
is no longer the same young girl
et cetera. Alas.

God was at last to believe in man:
good and strong.
But good and strong
are still two different people.

How to live—someone asked me in a letter,
someone I had wanted
to ask the same thing.

Again and as always,
and as seen above
there are no questions more urgent
than the naive ones.

Children of Our Era

We are children of our era;
our era is political.

All affairs, day and night,
yours, ours, theirs,
are political affairs.

Like it or not,
your genes have a political past,
your skin a political cast,
your eyes a political aspect.

What you say has a resonance;
what you are silent about is telling.
Either way, it's political.

Even when you head for the hills
you're taking political steps
on political ground.

Even apolitical poems are political,
and above us shines the moon,
by now no longer lunar.
To be or not to be, that is the question.
Question? What question? Dear, here's a suggestion:
a political question.

You don't even have to be a human being
to gain political significance.
Crude oil will do,
or concentrated feed, or any raw material.

Or even a conference table whose shape
was disputed for months:
should we negotiate life and death
at a round table or a square one?

Meanwhile people were dying,
animals perishing,
houses burning,
and fields growing wild,
just as in times most remote
and less political.

Torture

Nothing has changed.
The body is painful,
it must eat, breathe air, and sleep,
it has thin skin, with blood right beneath,
it has a goodly supply of teeth and nails,
its bones are brittle, its joints extensible.
In torture, all this is taken into account.

Nothing has changed.
The body trembles, as it trembled
before and after the founding of Rome,
in the twentieth century before and after Christ.
Torture is, the way it's always been, only the earth has shrunk,
and whatever happens, feels like it's happening next door.

Nothing has changed.
Only there are more people,
and next to old transgressions, new ones have appeared,
real, alleged, momentary, none,
but the scream, the body's answer for them—
was, is, and always will be the scream of innocence,
in accord with the age-old scale and register.

Nothing has changed.
Except maybe manners, ceremonies, dances.
Yet the gesture of arms shielding the head
has remained the same.
The body writhes, struggles, and tries to break free.
Bowled over, it falls, draws in its knees,
bruises, swells, drools, and bleeds.

Nothing has changed.
Except for the courses of rivers,
the contours of forests, seashores, deserts, and icebergs.
Among these landscapes the poor soul winds,
vanishes, returns, approaches, recedes.
A stranger to itself, evasive,
at one moment sure, the next unsure of its existence,
while the body is and is and is
and has no place to go.

The End and the Beginning

After every war
someone has to clean up.
Things won't
straighten themselves up, after all.

Someone has to push the rubble
to the side of the road,
so the corpse-filled wagons
can pass.

Someone has to get mired
in scum and ashes,
sofa springs,
splintered glass,
and bloody rags.

Someone has to drag in a girder
to prop up a wall,
Someone has to glaze a window,
rehang a door.

Photogenic it's not,
and takes years.
All the cameras have left
for another war.

We'll need the bridges back,
and new railway stations.
Sleeves will go ragged
from rolling them up.

Someone, broom in hand,
still recalls the way it was.
Someone else listens
and nods with unsevered head.
But already there are those nearby
starting to mill about
who will find it dull.

From out of the bushes
sometimes someone still unearths
rusted-out arguments
and carries them to the garbage pile.

Those who knew
what was going on here
must make way for
those who know little.
And less than little.
And finally as little as nothing.

In the grass that has overgrown
causes and effects,
someone must be stretched out
blade of grass in his mouth
gazing at the clouds.

Hatred

Look how spry it still is,
how well it holds up:
hatred, in our century.
How lithely it takes high hurdles.
How easy for it to pounce, to seize.

It is not like other feelings.
Both older and younger than they are.
It alone gives birth to causes
which rouse it to life.
If it sleeps, it's never for eternity.
Insomnia doesn't sap its strength—it boosts it.

Religion or no religion—
as long as it kneels at the start
Motherland or fatherland—
as long as it's in the race.
Even justice is good enough to start with.
After that it speeds off on its own.
Hatred. Hatred.
The grimace of love's ecstasy
twists its face.

Oh, those other feelings,
so sickly and sluggish.
Since when could brotherhood
count on milling crowds?
Was compassion ever first across the finish line?
How many followers does doubt command?
Only hatred commands, for hatred's got it down.

Smart, able, hardworking.
Need we say how many songs it has written?
How many pages of history it has numbered?
How many human carpets it has unrolled
over how many plazas and stadiums?

Let's face it:
Hatred can create beauty.
Marvelous are its fire-glows, in deep night.
Clouds of smoke most beautiful, at rosy dawn.
It's hard to deny ruins their pathos
and not to see bawdy humor
in the stout column poking out of them.

It is a master of contrast
between clatter and silence,
red blood and white snow.
Above all the image of a clean-shaven torturer
standing over his defiled victim
never bores it.

It is always ready for new tasks.
If it has to wait, it waits.
They say hatred is blind. Blind?
With eyes sharp as a sniper's,
it looks bravely into the future
—alone.

translated by Joanna Trzeciak and Marek Lugowski

Reality Demands

Reality demands
we also state the following:
life goes on.
At Cannae and Borodino,
at Kosovo Polje and in Guernica.

There is a gas station
in a small plaza in Jericho,
and freshly painted
benches near Bila Hora.
Letters travel
between Pearl Harbor and Hastings,
a furniture truck passes
before the eyes of the lion of Chaeronea,
and only an atmospheric front advances
toward the blossoming orchards near Verdun.

There is so much of Everything,
that Nothing is quite well concealed.
Music flows
from yachts at Actium
and on board couples dance in the sun.

So much keeps happening,
that it must be happening everywhere.
Where not a stone is left standing,
there is an ice-cream truck
besieged by children.

Where Hiroshima had been,
Hiroshima is again
manufacturing products
for everyday use.

Not without its draws is this terrible world,
not without its dawns
worth our waking.

In the fields of Maciejowice
the grass is green
and on the grass is—you know how grass is—
transparent dew.

Maybe there are no fields but battlefields,
those still remembered,
and those long forgotten,
birch groves and cedar groves,
snows and sands, iridescent swamps,
and ravines of dark defeat
where today, in sudden need,
you squat behind a bush.

What moral flows from this? Probably none.
But what really flows is quickly drying blood,
and as always, some rivers and clouds.

On the tragic mountain passes
the wind blows hats off heads
and we cannot help—
but laugh.

Some People

Some people fleeing some other people.
In some country under the sun
and some clouds.

They leave behind some of their everything,
sown fields, some chickens, dogs,
mirrors in which fire now sees itself reflected.

On their backs are pitchers and bundles,
the emptier, the heavier from one day to the next.

Taking place stealthily is somebody's stopping,
and in the commotion, somebody's bread somebody's snatching
and a dead child somebody's shaking.

In front of them some still not the right way,
nor the bridge that should be
over a river strangely rosy.
Around them, some gunfire, at times closer, at times farther off,
and, above, a plane circling somewhat.

Some invisibility would come in handy,
some grayish stoniness,
or even better, non-being
for a little or a long while.

Something else is yet to happen, only where and what?
Someone will head toward them, only when and who,
in how many shapes and with what intentions?
Given a choice,
maybe he will choose not to be the enemy
and leave them with some kind of life.

. . . I knock at the door of the rock . . .

Circus Animals

Bears are stomping in perfect time.
A lion jumps through flaming hoops.
A whip cracks and the music grinds.
A monkey rides a bike in a yellow suit.
A whip cracks and the animals turn their glance.
Dogs dance in carefully measured movement.
An elephant walks with a pitcher in perfect balance.

Myself, I'm quite embarrassed, I, a human.

People didn't enjoy themselves that day.
You wouldn't know it from the clapping hands
though one hand elongated by a whip
cast a striking shadow on the sand.

Water

A raindrop fell on my hand,
crafted from the Ganges and the Nile,

from the ascended frost of a seal's whiskers,
from water in broken pots in the cities of Ys and Tyre.

On my index finger
the Caspian Sea isn't landlocked,

and the Pacific flows meekly into the Rudava,
the one that flew in a cloud over Paris

in seventeen sixty-four
on the seventh of May at three in the morning.

There are not enough lips to pronounce
your transient names, O water.

I would have to say them in every language
pronouncing all the vowels at once,

at the same time keeping silent—for the sake of a lake
that waited in vain for a name,

and is no longer on earth—as it is in the heavens,
whose stars are no longer reflected in it.

Someone was drowning; someone dying
called out for you. That was long ago and yesterday.

You extinguished houses; you carried them off
like trees, forests like cities.

You were in baptismal fonts and in the bathtubs of courtesans,
in kisses, in shrouds.

Eating away at stones, fueling rainbows.
In the sweat and dew of pyramids and lilacs.

How light all this is in the raindrop.
How delicately the world touches me.

Whenever wherever whatever has happened
is written on the waters of Babel.

Conversation with a Rock

I knock at the door of the rock.
"It's me, let me in.
I want to enter your interior,
have a look around,
take you in like breath."

"Go away," says the rock,
"I am shut tight.
Even broken to bits
we would be shut tight.
Even ground into sand
we would not let anyone in."

I knock at the door of the rock.
"It's me, let me in.
I come out of sheer curiosity.
Life is my only chance.
I plan on wandering through your palace,
and then touring the leaf and the water droplet.
I don't have too much time for all this.
My mortality ought to move you."

"I'm a rock," says the rock,
"I can't help but be grave.
Go away.
I lack the muscles for laughing."

I knock at the door of the rock.
"It's me, let me in.
I've heard there are vast, empty rooms inside you,
unseen, beautiful in vain,
mute, devoid of the echo of footsteps.
Admit it, you don't know much about any of this."

"Vast, empty rooms," says the rock,
"but there is no room in them.
Beautiful maybe, but not suited to the taste
Of your meager senses.
You may get to know me, but you will never know me.
I turn my whole surface to you,
and turn my entire interior away."

I knock at the door of the rock.
"It's me, let me in.
I'm not seeking shelter for eternity.
I'm not unhappy.
I'm not homeless.
My world is worth returning to.
I'll enter and leave empty-handed.
And as evidence that I was truly present
I'll offer nothing but words,
which no one will believe."

"You will not be coming in," says the rock.
"You lack a sense of partaking.
None of your senses can make up for the sense of partaking.
Even sight, sharpened to omnividence,
will get you nowhere without a sense of partaking.
You will not be coming in. You have but a scent of this sense,
merely its seed, imagination.

I knock at the door of the rock.
"It's me, let me in.
I can't wait two thousand centuries
to come in under your roof."

"If you don't believe me," says the rock,
"go to the leaf, you'll hear the same thing.
Or to the water droplet; it'll say the same.
Finally, ask a hair from your own head.
I am bursting with laughter, laughter, giant laughter
though I don't know how to laugh."

I knock at the door of the rock.
"It's me, let me in."

"I don't have a door," says the rock.

Birds Returning

Again this spring the birds returned too early.
Rejoice reason, instinct too can err.
It has a lapse, an oversight—and they fall into the snow,
and perish badly, perish in a manner
unbefitting their well-wrought throats and superclaws,
reliable cartilage, and conscientious membranes,
river basins of heart, labyrinths of entrails,
naves of ribs and vertebrae in glorious enfilade,
feathers worthy of their own pavilion in a museum of fine crafts,
and a beak of monastic patience.

This is no dirge, but merely indignation,
that an angel made of real protein,
a kite with glands straight out of the Songs of Songs,
singular in air, uncountable in hand,
tissue after tissue bound into a unity
of time and place as in classical drama,
to the applause of wings,
falls and lays itself to rest by a stone,
which in its own archaic and crude way
sees life as a string of failed attempts.

Seen from Above

A dead beetle lies on a dirt road.
Three pairs of legs are neatly folded across its belly.
Instead of the chaos of death—tidiness and order.
The horror of the sight is moderate,
the scope strictly local from crabgrass to peppermint.
Sorrow is not contagious. The sky is blue.

For our peace of mind, animals do not pass away,
but die a seemingly shallower death
losing—we'd like to believe—fewer feelings and less world,
exiting—or so it seems—a less tragic stage.
Their meek souls do not scare us at night,
they value distance,
they know their place.

So here it is: the dead beetle in the road
gleams unlamented at the sun.
A glance at it would be as good as a thought:
it seems that nothing important happened here.
Important supposedly applies only to us.
Only to our life, only to our death,
a death which enjoys a forced right of way.

View with a Grain of Sand

We call it a grain of sand.
But it calls itself neither grain nor sand.
It does fine without a name
general, specific,
transient, permanent,
mistaken, or apt.

Our glance, our touch do nothing for it.
It does not feel seen or touched.
Its falling onto the windowsill
is only our adventure.
It might as well be falling on anything,
not knowing whether it's already landed,
or is still in free fall.

Out the window there's a beautiful view of a lake,
but this sight does not see itself.
Colorless and shapeless,
soundless, odorless,
and painless is this world to it.

To the bottom of the lake, it's bottomless,
and shoreless to its shore.
To its waters, neither dry nor wet.
Neither singular nor plural are the waves that whoosh,
deaf to their own whooshing
around stones neither small nor large.

And all this is happening under a sky, skyless by nature,
in which the sun goes down, without going down at all,
hiding without hiding behind an unwitting cloud,
which the wind thrashes for no other reason
than that it's blowing.

One second passes.
A second second.
A third.
But these are only our three seconds.

Time ran by like a courier with an urgent message.
But that's just our simile.
A made-up character, implanted haste,
and message inhuman.

Sky

The sky is where we should have started.
Window without a sill, without a frame, without a pane.
An opening wide open, with nothing
beyond it.

I don't have to wait for a starry night,
nor crane my neck,
to look at the sky.
I have the sky at my back, close at hand and on my eyelids.
It is the sky that wraps me tight
and lifts me from beneath.

The highest mountains
are no closer than the deepest
valleys to the sky.
No place has any more of it
than any other place.
A cloud is as ruthlessly
crushed by the sky as a grave is.
A mole is as high, sky high
as an owl beating its wings.
Whatever falls into the abyss,
falls from sky into sky.

Friable, fluid, rocky,
flammable, volatile stretches
of sky, specks of sky,
gusts of sky, heaps of sky.
Sky is omnipresent,
even in darkness under the skin.

I eat the sky, I excrete the sky.
I'm a trap in a trap,
an inhabited inhabitant,
an embrace embraced,
a question that answers a question.

Dividing earth and sky
is not the right way
to think about this wholeness.
It only allows one to live
at a more precise address—
were I to be searched for
I'd be found much faster.
My distinguishing marks
are rapture and despair.

Clouds

To describe the clouds
I would have to rush—
in but a split second
they're not what they were, they're different.

It's their nature
never to repeat
shapes, hues, poses, and formations.

Unburdened by the memory of anything,
they float effortlessly above the facts.

What kind of witnesses are they—
they drift apart in an instant.

Compared to clouds
life seems grounded,
nearly permanent and all but eternal.

Next to clouds
even a stone looks like a brother
you can depend on,
while they are, well, distant and flighty cousins.

Let people be, if they want to,
and then each of them dies in turn.
To them, the clouds, none of this
is of any concern;
indeed, it's very strange.

Over your entire life,
and mine, not entire yet,
they parade in splendor as they have from the outset.

They are not bound to perish with us when we die.
They don't have to be seen to fly.

In Abundance

I am who I am.
A coincidence as inscrutable
as any other.

Other ancestors
might have been mine, after all,
then from some other nest
I would have flown,
from some other stump
I would have crawled in my shell.

In nature's wardrobe
there are many costumes—
spider, seagull, field mouse.
Each fits like a glove from the get-go
and is loyally worn
until it wears out.

I, too, had no choice,
but I can't complain.
I could have been someone
much less singular.
Someone from a school of fish,
from an anthill, from a buzzing swarm,
a piece of landscape thrashed by the wind.

Someone much less lucky,
bred for fur
or for a holiday meal,
something swimming under a cover glass.

A tree stuck in the earth,
with a fire approaching.

A blade of grass trampled by a run
of incomprehensible events.

One born under a dark cloud
whose lining gleams for others.

But what if I had awakened fear in people,
or merely revulsion,
or merely pity?

If I hadn't been born
into the right tribe and
paths closed before me?

Fate has proved
benevolent so far.

The memory of good moments
might not have been granted me.

A penchant for comparisons
might have been withheld from me.

I might have been myself—though without the wonder,
but that would have meant
being someone else.

The Silence of Plants

A one-sided relationship is developing quite well
between you and me.

I know what a leaf, petal, kernel, cone, and stem are,
and I know what happens to you in April and December.

Though my curiosity is unrequited,
I gladly stoop for some of you
and for others I crane my neck.

I have names for you:
maple, burdock, liverwort,
heather, juniper, mistletoe, and forget-me-not,
but you have none for me.

After all, we share a common journey.
When traveling together, it's normal to talk,
exchanging remarks, say, about the weather,
or about the stations flashing past.

We wouldn't run out of topics for so much connects us.
The same star keeps us in reach.
We cast shadows according to the same laws.
Both of us at least try to know something, each in our own way,
and even in what we don't know there lies a resemblance.

Just ask and I will explain as best I can:
what it is to see through eyes,
why my heart beats,
and how come my body is unrooted.

But how does someone answer questions never posed
when on top of that
she is such an utter nobody to you?

Undergrowth, shrubbery, meadows, and rushes—
everything I say to you is a monologue,
and it is not you who's listening.

A conversation with you is necessary and impossible,
urgent in a hurried life
and postponed for never.

. . . of human kind for now . . .

A Note

In the first display
we have a stone.
Please note
the indistinct scratch.
The work of chance,
some might say.

In the second display
we have the remains of a cranium.
Animal or human—
it's hard to tell.
A bone is a bone.
Let's move on.
There's nothing here.

Only an ancient
resemblance remains
between the spark struck from stone
and a star.
Drawn for centuries
the space of comparison
has been well preserved.

That was the thing
that lured us out of the depths of our kind,
led us out of the realm of dreams,
from before there was a word dream,
in which what is alive
is born forever
and dies without death.

That was the thing
that turned our head to a human one,
spark to star,
one to many,
each to all,
temple to temple
and what it opened in us
does not have eyelids.

Out of the stone
the sky flew.
A stick branched out
into a thicket of ends.
A snake raised the sting
from the tangle of its reasons.
Time staggered
in the rings of trees.
Multiplied in the echo
was the wailing of the awakened.

In the first display
there is a stone.
In the second display
the remains of a cranium.
The animals lost us.
Whom will we lose?
Through what kind of resemblance?
What compared to what?

The Cave

Nothing on the walls,
only moisture trickles down.
It's cold and dark here.

But cold and dark
after an extinguished fire.
Nothing—but the nothing left of a bison
painted in ochre.

Nothing—but a nothing left
after the long resistance
of an animal's bent neck.
So, a Beautiful Nothing.
Worthy of a capital letter.
A heresy against commonplace nothingness,
unconverted and proud of the difference.

Nothing—but after us,
who were here
and ate our own hearts,
and drank our own blood.

Nothing, that is, our
unfinished dance.
First time by the fire
your thighs, hands, necks, faces.
My first holy bellies
full of tiny Pascals.

Silence—but after voices.
Not a silence of the sluggish sort.
A silence that once had its own throats,
pipes and drums.
Grafted here like a wilding
by howling and laughter.

Silence—but in a darkness
exalted by eyelids.
Darkness—but in a chill
to the skin, to the bone.
Chill—but that of death.

On earth, maybe the only one
in the heavens? seventh heaven?

You headed out of emptiness
and you truly want to know.

A Speech at the Lost and Found

I lost a few goddesses on my way from south to north,
as well as many gods on my way from east to west.
Some stars went out on me for good: part for me, O sky.
Island after island collapsed into the sea on me.
I'm not sure exactly where I left my claws,
who wears my fur, who dwells in my shell.
My siblings died out when I crawled onto land
and only a tiny bone in me marks the anniversary.
I leapt out of my skin, squandered vertebrae and legs,
and left my senses many many times.
Long ago I closed my third eye to it all,
waved it off with my fins, shrugged my branches.

Scattered by the four winds to a place that time forgot,
how little there remains of me surprises me a lot,
a singular being of human kind for now,
who lost her umbrella in a tram somehow.

A Large Number

Four billion people on this earth,
but my imagination is the way it's always been:
bad with large numbers.
It is still moved by particularity.
It flits about the darkness like a flashlight beam,
disclosing only random faces,
while the rest go blindly by,
unthought of, unpitied.
Not even a Dante could have stopped that.
So what do you do when you're not,
even with all the muses on your side?

Non omnis moriar—a premature worry.
Yet am I fully alive, and is that enough?
It never has been, and even less so now.
I select by rejecting, for there's no other way,
but what I reject, is more numerous,
more dense, more intrusive than ever.
At the cost of untold losses—a poem, a sigh.
I reply with a whisper to a thunderous calling.
How much I am silent about I can't say.
A mouse at the foot of mother mountain.
Life lasts as long as a few lines of claws in the sand.

My dreams—even they are not as populous as they should be.
There is more solitude in them than crowds or clamor.
Sometimes someone long dead will drop by for a bit.
A single hand turns a knob.
Annexes of echo overgrow the empty house.
I run from the threshold down into the quiet
valley, seemingly no one's—an anachronism by now.

Where does all this space still in me come from—
that I don't know.

Surplus

A new star has been discovered,
which doesn't mean it's gotten any brighter
or something missing has been gained.

The star is large and distant,
so distant, that it's small,
even smaller than others
a lot smaller than itself.
Surprise would be nothing surprising
if we only had time for it.

Star's age, star's mass, star's position,
all of that may be enough
for one doctoral thesis
and a modest glass of wine
in the circles close to the sky:
an astronomer, his wife, relatives, and colleagues,
a casual ambience, no dress code,
local topics fuel a down-to-earth conversation
and people are munching on terra chips.

A wonderful star,
but that's still no reason
not to drink to the ladies,
incomparably closer.

Star without consequences.
Without influence on weather, fashion, the score of the game,
changes in government, income, or the crisis of values.

With no effect on propaganda or heavy industry.
Without reflection in the finish of the conference table.
An excess number for life's numbered days.

Why need we ask
under how many stars someone is born
and under how many they die a little while later?

A new one.
"At least show me where it is."
"Between the edge of that jagged grayish cloud
and the twig of that locust tree on the left."
"Oh," I say.

On Death, without Exaggeration

It can't tell a joke
from a star, from a bridge,
from weaving, from mining, from farming,
from shipbuilding, or baking.

When we're discussing our future plans
it's got to get in the final word,
off the topic.

It doesn't even know the things
directly tied to its trade:
digging graves,
assembling coffins,
cleaning up after itself.

So busy killing
it's doing it badly,
without system or skill.
As if it were just learning on each of us.

Triumphs aside
how about the defeats,
the missed blows
and second tries.

At times it lacks the strength
to swat a fly out of the air.
To many a caterpillar
it's lost a crawling race.

These bulbs, pods,
feelers, fins, tracheae,
nuptial plumage, and winter fur
all testify to a backlog
in its slothful work.

Ill will does not suffice
and even our help during wars and coups d'état
is too little so far.

Hearts are pounding in eggs.
The skeletons of infants are growing.
Seeds are sprouting their first two leaves,
and often even tall trees on the horizon.

Whoever insists that it is omnipotent
is himself living proof
that omnipotent it's not.

There is no life that
couldn't be immortal,
if only for a split second.

Death
always arrives that split second late.

In vain it rattles the knob
of the invisible door.
However much one has gotten done,
that much it cannot take away.

No Title Required

It's all come down to me sitting under a tree
on a river bank
on a sunny morning.
It's an inconsequential event
that won't go down in history.
This is not a battle or a pact,
whose motives are examined,
or the notable assassination of a tyrant.

Yet I am sitting by the river; that's a fact.
And since I'm here,
I must have come from somewhere,
and before that
I must have turned up in many other places,
just like the conquerors of lands
before they set sail.

A moment, however fleeting, has a flamboyant past:
its Friday before its Saturday,
its May before its June.
Its horizons are as real
as those in the fieldglass of a commander.

This tree is a poplar, rooted here for years.
This river is the Raba, which didn't spring up yesterday.
The trail through the bushes
wasn't blazed the day before.
To disperse the clouds,
the wind must have blown them in earlier.

And though nothing special is happening nearby,
that doesn't mean the world is lacking for detail.
It's no less justified, nor more weakly defined,
than when the peopling of the continents held it captive.

It's not just conspiracies that are accompanied by silence,
not just coronations that have their procession of reasons.
The years of revolutionary anniversaries are rounded off
like stones on the beach.

Dense and intricate is the embroidery of circumstance.
An ant's stitch in the grass.
Grass sewn into the earth.
The pattern of a wave through which a stick threads its way.

It turns out that I am, and am looking.
Above me a white butterfly flits about in the air,
his wings belonging only to him,
and through my hands, a shadow flies,
none other, no one else's, than his own.

Facing such a view always leaves me uncertain
that the important
is more important than the unimportant.

One Version of Events

If indeed we were allowed to choose,
we must have been mulling things over for a long time.

The bodies offered us were uncomfortable
and wore out dreadfully.

The means of satisfying hunger
sickened us.
The passive inheritance of traits
and the tyranny of organs
put us off.

The world that was meant to surround us,
was in endless decay.
The effects of causes wreaked heavy havoc on it.

Of all those fates
given to us for inspection
most we rejected
in sorrow and horror.

Questions arose such as these:
what use is there in the painful delivery
of a dead child?
And why be a sailor
who never reaches port?

We agreed to death
but not in every form.
Love attracted us,
sure, but a love
that kept its word.

The fickleness of judgments
and impermanence of masterpieces
scared us off
from the service of art.

Everyone wanted a homeland without neighbors
and to live their entire lives
in an interval between wars.

None of us wanted to seize power
or be subject to it,
none of us wanted to fall victim
to our own delusions or anyone else's.
There were no volunteers
for tight crowds, parades,
and even less so for vanishing tribes;
but without them, history
never would have been able to march on
through centuries foreseen.

Meanwhile a goodly number
of lighted stars
had gone out and grown cold.
It was high time for a decision.

After many reservations
there finally appeared a few candidates
for discoverers and healers,
for philosophers without acclaim,
for several anonymous gardeners,
musicians and conjurers
—though for want of other submissions
even these lives
couldn't be fulfilled.

The whole thing
had to be rethought yet again.

We were offered
a package tour,
a journey from which we'd return
fast and for sure.

A chance to remain outside eternity,
which is, after all, monotonous
and ignorant of the concept of passing,
might never have come again.

We were riddled with doubt
whether, knowing it all beforehand,
we indeed knew it all.

Is such a premature choice
any choice at all?
Wouldn't it be better
to let it pass?
And if we are to choose,
to make the choice there?

We took a look at Earth.
Some adventurers were living there already.
A feeble plant
was clinging to a rock
with reckless trust
that the wind would not uproot it.

A smallish animal
was crawling out of its nook
with an effort and a hope that surprised us.

We found ourselves too cautious,
small-minded, and ridiculous.

Anyway, soon our numbers began to fade.
The least patient ones went off somewhere.
Theirs was a trial by fire
—that much was clear.
Indeed, they were lighting one
on the steep bank of a real river.

Several
were already heading back.
But not our way.
And as if they were carrying the spoils? Of what?

A Word on Statistics

Out of every hundred people

those who always know better:
fifty-two.

Unsure of every step:
nearly all the rest.

Ready to help,
as long as it doesn't take long:
forty-nine.

Always good,
because they cannot be otherwise:
four—well, maybe five.

Able to admire without envy:
eighteen.

Led to error
by youth (which passes):
sixty, plus or minus.

Those not to be messed with:
forty and four.

Living in constant fear
of someone or something:
seventy-seven.

Capable of happiness:
twenty-some-odd at most.

Harmless alone,
turning savage in crowds:
more than half, for sure.

Cruel
when forced by circumstances:
it's better not to know
not even approximately.

Wise in hindsight:
not many more
than wise in foresight.

Getting nothing out of life but things:
thirty
(although I would like to be wrong).

Doubled over in pain,
without a flashlight in the dark:
eighty-three,
sooner or later.

Those who are just:
quite a few at thirty-five.

But if it takes effort to understand:
three.

Worthy of empathy:
ninety-nine.

Mortal:
one hundred out of one hundred—
a figure that has never varied yet.

... the unthinkable is thinkable ...

Atlantis

They did or did not exist.
On an island or not.
The ocean or not the ocean
swallowed them up or didn't.

Was there anyone to love anyone?
Was there anyone to fight anyone?
All or nothing happened
there or not there.

Seven cities stood there.
Is that for sure?
Intended to stand there forever.
Where's the evidence?

No they didn't invent the wheel.
Yes, they did invent the wheel.

Presumed. Dubious.
Uncommemorated.

Never pulled out of the air,
or fire, or water, or earth.

Never contained in stone
nor in a raindrop.

Never fit to stand
as a serious warning.

A meteorite fell.
It wasn't a meteorite.
A volcano erupted.
It wasn't a volcano.
Someone was shouting something.
No one, nothing.

On this plus-or-minus Atlantis.

In Heraclitus' River

In Heraclitus' river
a fish fishes for fish,
a fish quarters a fish with a sharp fish,
a fish builds a fish, a fish lives in a fish,
a fish flees a fish under siege.

In Heraclitus' river
a fish loves a fish,
your eyes—it says—glitter like fishes in the sky,
I want to swim with you to the common sea,
O most beautiful of the school of fish.

In Heraclitus' river
a fish invented the fish beyond fishes,
a fish kneels before the fish, a fish sings to the fish,
asks the fish for an easier swim.

In Heraclitus' river
I, the sole fish, I, a fish apart
(say, from the tree fish and the stone fish)
at certain moments find myself writing small fish
in scales so briefly silver,
that it may be the darkness winking in embarrassment.

A Poem in Honor Of

Once, upon a time, invented zero.
In an uncertain country. Under a star
which may be dark by now. Bounded by dates,
but no one would swear to them. Without a name,
not even a contentious one. Leaving behind
no golden words beneath his zero
about life being like. Nor any legends:
that one day he appended zero
to a picked rose and tied it up into a bouquet;
that when he was about to die, he rode off into the desert
on a hundred-humped camel; that he fell asleep
in the shadow of the palm of primacy; that he will awaken
when everything has been counted,
down to the last grain of sand. What a man.
Slipping into the fissure between fact and fiction,
he has escaped our notice. Resistant
to every fate. He sheds
every form I give him.
Silence has closed over him, his voice leaving no scar.
The absence has taken on the look of the horizon.
Zero writes itself.

Pursuit

I know that silence will greet me, but still.
No hubbub, no trumpets, no applause, but still.
Neither bells of alarm, nor alarm itself.

I can't even count on the slightest trace,
let alone silver palaces and gardens,
venerable elders, equitable laws,
wisdom in a crystal ball, but still.

I understand I'm not walking on the Moon
to look for rings, or for lost ribbons.
They always grab everything in time.

There's nothing to indicate.
Trash, junk, peels, shreds, crumbs,
shrapnel, shavings, shards, scraps, rubble.

All I can do is stoop and pick up a pebble
which isn't going to tell me where they went.
They don't like leaving me any cues.
In the art of erasing evidence, they are unrivaled.

I have long known their talent for vanishing in time,
their divine ability to elude grasp by horn, by tail,
by the hem of a gown billowing in flight.
I will never touch a hair on their heads.

Everywhere more cunning than I am by a single thought,
always one step ahead of me before I even get there,
sneeringly exposed to the hardships of being the first.

They don't exist, they never did, but still
time and again I have to repeat that to myself,
and try to quell my childish imaginings.

Yet what leapt so suddenly from underfoot
did not leap far, for when stepped on, it fell,
and though it wriggles still,
and emits a prolonged silence,
it is but a shadow, too much my own to feel I've reached my goal.

Interview with a Child

The master hasn't been among us long.
That's why he lurks in every corner.
He covers his face with his hands and peers through the gap.
Standing, forehead to the wall, he suddenly turns.

The master rejects with distaste the absurd thought
that a table lost from view must remain a table,
that the chair behind his back stays within the boundaries of a chair
without even trying to take advantage of the situation.

True, it's hard to catch the world in its otherness.
The apple tree returns to the window before you can bat an eye.
The rainbow-colored sparrows always darken just in time.
The handle, the pitcher's ear, will catch any murmur.
The nighttime closet feigns the passivity of the daytime closet.
The drawer tries to convince the master
that all that's in there is what was put in earlier.
Even when a book of fairy tales is suddenly opened,
the princess always gets to her seat in the picture.

They sense a newcomer in me—the master sighs—
they don't want to let a stranger play with them.
But how come everything that exists
is forced to exist in only one way
in a miserable state, with no escape from itself,
without pause or change of pace? In the humble here-to-there?
A fly trapped in a fly? A mouse trapped in a mouse?
A dog never turned loose from its hidden chain?
A fire, without the nerve to do anything
but burn the master's trusting finger a second time?
Is this the true ultimate world:
scattered wealth impossible to gather,
useless splendor, forbidden possibility?

No!—the master shouts and stomps all the feet
he can muster—in such enormous despair,
that even the six legs of a cricket would not suffice.

Nothing nothinged itself for me as well.
It truly turned itself inside out.
Where did I find myself?
From head to toe among the planets,
not even remembering how it was for me not to be.

O my dear that I met here and fell in love with here,
I can only imagine, with my hand on your shoulder,
how much emptiness is allotted us on the other side,
how much silence there for one cricket here,
how much meadow lacking there for a tiny leaf of sorrel here,
and the sun after darkness, like reparations
in a drop of dew—for such deep droughts there.

Starry helter-skelter! Here the other way around!
Stretched over curvature, weight, friction, and motion!
A break in infinity for the limitless sky!
A relief from non-space in the form of a swaying birch!

Now or never the wind moves a cloud
for the wind is exactly what doesn't blow there.
And a beetle steps onto a path in the dark suit of a witness
on the occasion of a long wait for a short life.

But it just so happens that I am with you.
And I really see nothing
ordinary about it.

Under a Certain Little Star

My apologies to chance for calling it necessity.
My apologies to necessity in case I'm mistaken.
Don't be angry, happiness, that I take you for my own.
May the dead forgive me that their memory's but a flicker.
My apologies to time for the quantity of world overlooked per
    second.
My apologies to an old love for treating a new one as the first.
Forgive me, far-off wars, for carrying my flowers home.
Forgive me, open wounds, for pricking my finger.
My apologies for the minuet record, to those calling out from the
    abyss.
My apologies to those in train stations for sleeping soundly at five
    in the morning.
Pardon me, hounded hope, for laughing sometimes.
Pardon me, deserts, for not rushing in with a spoonful of water.
And you, O hawk, the same bird for years in the same cage,
staring, motionless, always at the same spot,
absolve me even if you happen to be stuffed.
My apologies to the tree felled for four table legs.
My apologies to large questions for small answers.
Truth, do not pay me too much attention.
Solemnity, be magnanimous toward me.
Bear with me, O mystery of being, for pulling threads from your
    veil.
Soul, don't blame me that I've got you so seldom.
My apologies to everything that I can't be everywhere.
My apologies to all for not knowing how to be every man and
    woman.
I know that as long as I live nothing can excuse me,

since I am my own obstacle.

Do not hold it against me, O speech, that I borrow weighty words, and then labor to make them light.

The Dream of the Old Tortoise

The tortoise is dreaming of a leaf of lettuce
and suddenly next to the leaf springs to life
the Emperor, just as in times that predate us.
The tortoise doesn't know what a feat this betides.

The Emperor returned, not *in toto,* in truth,
in the form of quite shapely calves in white stockings
and a glimmer of sun off the black of his shoes.
The tortoise doesn't even know this is shocking.

Two legs on the stop from Jena to Austerlitz
and the roar of laughter lost above in the fog.
You could doubt the reality of any of this
and whether the Emperor's shoe is a brogue.

Right foot, left foot, it's difficult
to recognize somebody piecemeal.
The tortoise remembers but little from childhood
—as to whom he dreamt up, he is unclear.

Emperor or not. How does that information
affect the fact that in a tortoise's nap,
an unknown someone escaped nullification
and steals through the world! From heel to kneecap.

Pi

The admirable number pi:
three point one four one.
Every further digit is also just a start,
five nine two, for it never ends.
It can't be grasped, *six five three five,* at a glance,
eight nine, by calculation,
seven nine, through imagination,
or even *three two three eight* in jest, or by comparison
four six to anything
two six four three in the world.
The longest snake on earth ends at thirty-odd feet.
Same goes for fairy tale snakes, though they make it a little longer.
The caravan of digits that is pi
does not stop at the edge of the page,
but runs off the table and into the air
over the wall, a leaf, a bird's nest, the clouds, straight into the sky,
through all its bloatedness and bottomlessness.
O how short, all but mouse-like, is the comet's tail!
How frail is a ray of starlight, bending in any old space!
Meanwhile *two three fifteen three hundred nineteen*
my phone number your shirt size
the year nineteen seventy-three sixth floor
number of inhabitants sixty-five cents
hip measurement two fingers a charade and a code,
in which we find *how blithe the throstle sings!*
and *please remain calm,*
and *heaven and earth shall pass away,*
but not pi, that won't happen,
it still has an okay *five,*

and quite a fine *eight,*
an all but final *seven,*
prodding and prodding a plodding eternity
to last.

Miracle Fair

Commonplace miracle:
that so many commonplace miracles happen.

An ordinary miracle:
in the dead of night
the barking of invisible dogs.

One miracle out of many:
a small, airy cloud
yet it can block a large and heavy moon.

Several miracles in one:
an alder tree reflected in the water,
and that it's backwards left to right
and that it grows there, crown down
and never reaches the bottom,
even though the water is shallow.

An everyday miracle:
winds weak to moderate
turning gusty in storms.

First among equal miracles:
cows are cows.

Second to none:
just this orchard
from just that seed.

A miracle without a cape and top hat:
scattering white doves.

A miracle, for what else could you call it:
today the sun rose at three-fourteen
and will set at eight-o-one.

A miracle, less surprising than it should be:
even though the hand has fewer than six fingers,
it still has more than four.

A miracle, just take a look around:
the world is everywhere.

An additional miracle, as everything is additional:
the unthinkable
is thinkable.

. . . Oh Muse . . .

Leaving the Cinema

Dreams flickered on a white cloth.
Two hours in the shadow of the moon.
A happy return from a journey.
Love set to a sentimental tune.

After the fairy tale the world is black and blue and veiled in mist.
Here faces and roles go uninstructed.
The girl acts out her many woes
and the young soldier sings out his.

I return to you, to the real world,
crowded and dark, full of fate:
to you, a girl looking in vain
and a one-armed youth, at a wrought-iron gate.

Rubens' Women

Herculasses, a feminine fauna.
Naked as the crashing of barrels.
Cooped up atop trampled beds.
They sleep with mouths poised to crow.
Their pupils have retreated into the depths,
and penetrate to the heart of their glands,
trickling yeast into their blood.

Daughters of the Baroque. Dough bloats in a bowl,
baths are steaming, wines are blushing,
piglets of cloud are dashing across the sky,
trumpets neigh in physical alarm.

O pumpkinned, O excessive ones,
doubled by your unveiling,
trebled by your violent poses,
fat love dishes.

Their skinny sisters got up earlier,
before dawn broke within the painting,
and no one saw them walking single file
on the unpainted side of the canvas.

Exiles of style. Ribs all counted.
Birdlike feet and hands.
They try to ascend on gaunt shoulderblades.

The thirteenth century would have given them a golden backdrop.
The twentieth, a silver screen.
But the seventeenth has nothing for the flat-chested.

For even the sky curves in relief—
curvaceous angels, a curvaceous god—
a moustached Apollo astride a sweaty steed
enters the steaming bedchamber.

Poetry Reading

Oh muse, not to be a boxer is not to be at all.
You shorted us a roaring crowd.
Only twelve have trickled in
and yet it's time that we begin.
Half are here because it's raining;
the rest are relatives. Oh muse.

The ladies would swoon and faint but here's the catch:
they'd do it, but only at a boxing match,
the place where such Dantesque scenes are allowed,
not to mention the ascent to heaven. Oh muse.

Not to be a boxer, but a poet,
to be sentenced to the ranks of the heavyBlakes,
for lack of muscles, to display before the world
what might become assigned reading—if fate should be so
    generous—
Oh muse. Oh Pegasus,
equine angel.

In the front row an old man just entered la-la-land,
and dreams his wife has come back from the grave and
is baking him a cake with plums.
With a bit of fire but not too much or else the cake might burn
we start the reading. Oh muse.

The Joy of Writing

Where is the written doe headed, through these written woods?
To drink from the written spring
that copies her muzzle like carbon paper?
Why is she raising her head, does she hear something?
Perched on four legs borrowed from the truth
she pricks up her ears from under my fingertips.
Silence—even this word rustles across the page
and parts the branches
stemming from the word "woods."

Above the blank page, poised to pounce, lurk
letters, which might spell trouble,
penning sentences
from which there will be no escape.

There is, in an ink drop, a goodly supply
of hunters, eyes winked,
ready to charge down this steep pen,
circle the doe, and sight their guns.

They forget there is no life here.
Different laws, black and white, hold sway.
The blink of an eye will last as long as I want,
allowing division into little eternities
full of bullets stopped in mid-flight.
Nothing will happen forever here if I say so.
Not even a leaf will fall without my go-ahead,
nor will a blade of grass bend under the full stop of the hoof.

Then is there such a world
where I wield fate unfettered?
A time I bind with strings of signs?
Existence without end at my command?

The joy of writing.
The prospect of preserving.
Revenge of a mortal hand.

Landscape

In an old master's landscape
trees take root beneath the oil paint,
the path clearly leads somewhere,
a dignified blade of grass replaces the signature,
it's a credible five o'clock in the afternoon,
a gently but firmly stopped May,
so I too have stopped off—yes, dear,
I am that maiden beneath the ash tree.

Look how far away I've moved from you,
how white is my bonnet, how yellow my skirt,
how firmly I clutch my basket so I won't fall out of the painting,
how I parade in another's fate
and take a rest from living mysteries.

Even if you called, I would not hear,
and even if I heard, I would not turn,
and even if I made that impossible move,
your face would seem strange to me.

I know the world within a six-mile radius.
I know the herbs and spells for every ailment.
God still looks down on the top of my head.
I still pray for an unsudden death.
War is a punishment, and peace a reward.
Embarrassing dreams come from Satan.
My soul is as plain as the pit of a plum.

I don't know the game of hearts.
I don't know the nakedness of the father of my children.
I don't suspect the Song of Songs
of a complex, inked-up first draft.
What I want to say, is in complete sentences.
I don't use despair, for it is not mine,
but only entrusted me for safekeeping.

Even if you barred my path,
even if you looked into my eyes,
I would pass you by on the razor's edge of the abyss.

To the right is my house, which I know my way around,
along with its stairs and the passageway in,
where unpainted stories unfold:
the cat leaps onto a bench,
the sun falls onto a tin pitcher,
and a gaunt man sits at the table
repairing a clock.

Thomas Mann

Dear mermaids, this is how it had to be,
beloved fauns, honorable angels,
evolution has firmly disowned you.
It doesn't lack imagination, yet you and your
fins from the Devonian depths, but breasts from the alluvium,
fingered hands, yet cloven feet,
arms, not instead of, but in addition to wings,
these, shudder to think, vertebrette-bimorphlets,
untimely tailed, horned to be ornery,
but birdly on the sly, clusters and compoundings,
these jigsaw marjorie daws, these couplets
pairing man and heron with such bearing
that he soars and is immortal and knows all
—you have to admit, that would be a joke,
eternal overkill and endless bother,
which nature doesn't go to, doesn't want, and never will.

Good thing it at least permits a certain fish to fly
with provocative expertise. Each such ascent
is a consolation for the rules, a pardon
from universal necessity, a gift
more generous than needed for a world to be a world.

Good thing it at least allows such excessive scenes
as a duck-billed platypus nursing her chicks.
Nature could have objected—and who among us would have
   discovered
he had been robbed?
                        And best of all,
it overlooked the moment a mammal emerged,
his hand miraculously feathered by a fountain pen.

Stage Fright

Poets and writers,
or so it is said,
so poets aren't writers, then what are they—

Poets are poetry, writers are prose—

Prose can have anything, even poetry,
but poetry can have only poetry—

According to the poster announcing it
with a capital P in art nouveau filigree
written into the strings of a winged lyre,
I should have descended, not walked in—

And wouldn't it be better barefoot,
than in these cheap shoes
clomping, squeaking,
an awkward substitute for an angel—

If only this dress were longer, trailed more,
and the poems pulled not out of the purse, but thin air,
all done for effect, a fest, a bell-ringing day,
ding to dong
a b, a b, b a—

And on the platform already lurks a séance
table, sort of, on gilded legs
and on the table a lone candle smolders—

Which means
I will have to read by candlelight
what I've written by common bulb
tap tap tap on the typewriter—

Not worried ahead of time
whether it's poetry
or what kind of poetry—

Is it the kind where prose is inappropriate—
or the kind that's appropriate in prose—

And what is the difference
visible only in half-darkness
against the crimson curtain
with purple fringe?

A Great Man's House

It's written in marble in golden letters:
here the great man lived and worked and died.
He laid the gravel for these paths.
This bench—don't touch—he carved from stone himself.
And—careful, three steps—we're going inside.

He made it into the world at just the right time.
Everything that was to pass, passed in this house.
Not in a high-rise,
not in square footage, furnished yet empty,
among anonymous neighbors,
on some fifteenth floor,
where it's hard to drag school field trips.

In this room he ruminated,
in this alcove he slept,
and over here he entertained guests.
Portraits, an armchair, a desk, a pipe, a globe, a flute,
a worn-out rug, a sun room.
From here he exchanged nods with his tailor and shoemaker
who made his things to measure.

That's not the same as photographs in boxes,
dried-out pens in a plastic cup,
a store-bought wardrobe in a store-bought closet,
a window with a better view of clouds than people.

Happy? Unhappy?
That's not relevant here.
He still confided in his letters,
without thinking they would be opened on their way.

He still kept a detailed and honest diary,
without fearing he would lose it in a search.
The most he had to worry about was the coming of a comet.
The destruction of the world was only in God's hands.

He died, but luckily not in the hospital
behind some anonymous white screen.
There was still someone with him to remember
his muttered words.

As if he had been given
a reusable life:
he sent his books to be bound,
he wouldn't cross out the names of the dead from his address book.
And the trees he had planted in the garden behind the house
still grew for him as *Juglans regia*
and *Quercus rubra* and *Ulmus* and *Larix*
and *Fraxinus excelsior.*

People on the Bridge

Strange planet and strange people on it.
They yield to time, but don't want to recognize time.
They have their ways of expressing resistance.
They make pictures such as this:

Nothing remarkable at first glance.
One can see water,
one riverbank,
a narrow boat strenuously moving upstream,
a bridge over the water,
and people on the bridge.
They are clearly picking up the pace,
as rain starts lashing down from a dark cloud.

The point is, nothing happens further.
The cloud changes neither shape nor color.
The rain neither subsides nor surges.
The boat moves without moving.
The people on the bridge run
exactly where they ran before.

It is hard to get by without commentary:
This is not at all an innocent picture.
Time's been stopped here,
its laws no longer consulted.
It's been denied impact on the course of events,
disregarded and dishonored.

Thanks to a rebel,
one Hiroshige Utagawa
(a being who, by the way,
passed away, as is proper, long ago),
time stumbled and fell.

Perhaps it is merely a prank without much meaning,
a whim on the scale of just a few galaxies,
but just in case,
let's add what happens next:

For generations it has been considered in good taste
to hold this painting in high esteem,
to praise it and be greatly moved by it.

For some, even that is not enough.
They hear the patter of rain,
feel the chill of raindrops on necks and shoulders,
they look at the bridge and the people on it
as if they saw themselves there,
in that never-ending race
along the endless road, to be traveled for eternity
and they have the audacity to believe
that it is real.

Some Like Poetry

Some—
not all, that is.
Not even the majority of all, but the minority.
Not counting school, where one must,
or the poets themselves,
there'd be maybe two such people in a thousand.

Like—
but one also likes chicken-noodle soup,
one likes compliments and the color blue,
one likes an old scarf,
one likes to prove one's point,
one likes to pet a dog.

Poetry—
but what sort of thing is poetry?
Many a shaky answer
has been given to this question.
But I do not know and do not know and hold on to it,
as to a saving bannister.

Notes

. . . for a long time chance had been toying with them . . .

Commemoration

In the 1957 collection *Calling Out to Yeti* [Wołanie do Yeti] "Commemoration" follows "Openness." In the present collection this order has been reversed owing to a fondness for "Commemoration" shared by the author and the translator.

"Assumption in formal wear,": given the religious overtones of this poem, which is structured like a part of the Catholic liturgy called the Kyrie, here I chose to render the adjective *wniebowzięty* as the proper noun "Assumption." The Polish word has two meanings, the archaic literal meaning "taken to heaven," and the modern figurative meaning "rapturous, entranced." For more on the relationship between the natural and the religious in Szymborska, see notes to the poem "Sky."

The word "ornithogothic" in the penultimate stanza reflects Szymborska's coinage "early-bird gothic," which has an air of linguistic innovation in Polish, but bargain-basement connotations in English, hence the Latinate rendering was chosen here.

Openness
from the 1957 collection *Calling Out to Yeti* [Wołanie do Yeti]

The Swift of the third stanza is Jonathan Swift (1667–1745), the Anglo-Irish satirist, best known for *Gulliver's Travels* and "A Modest Proposal."

Drinking Wine
from the 1962 collection *Salt* [Sól]

The three ladies of the penultimate stanza each have their own creation myth. According to Genesis 2:21–23, God created Eve from Adam's rib. Venus (the Roman name for Aphrodite, the Greek goddess of love and beauty) was believed to have been born from the foam of the sea and is thus often depicted rising out of the water as in *The Birth of Venus* by Botticelli. Minerva (the Roman goddess known from Greek mythology as Athena), goddess of wisdom, is said to have sprung fully grown from the head of her father, Jove, known in Greek mythology as Zeus.

I am too close for him . . .
from the 1962 collection *Salt* [Sól]

"Not with my voice sings the fish in the net.": Here Szymborska alludes not to any particular piece of folklore, but rather evokes the folkloric spirit itself.

The three final lines of the poem hearken back to the medieval theological dispute over the corporeality of angels (including fallen ones). Although often attributed to Saint Thomas Aquinas, this alleged quibble was more plausibly a commonplace mockery of medieval disputes flowing from the pens of such writers as Isaac D'Israeli in his *Curiosities of Literature* (1791–1834).

A Dream
from the 1962 collection *Salt* [Sól]

"dead-in-battle . . .": refers to World War II. A few of the motifs here can be found in several Szymborska poems of the late 1940s: "Johnny the Fiddler" ("Janko Muzykant"), "All Souls Day" ("Zaduszki"), "Victory" ("Zwycięstwo"), and "The Return of Sorrow" ("Powrót żalu").

A Man's Household
An occasional poem written in the 1970s and presented as a birthday gift to Kornel Filipowicz, Szymborska's longtime companion, who died in 1990. This poem was first published in *Dekada Literacka* 3 (1996), and later reprinted in *NaGłos* 24 (1996).

"a Lake Mamry water hen's three feathers in a basket,": Lake Mamry is a sizable lake in the northeast of Poland.

A Thank-You Note
from the 1976 collection *A Large Number* [Wielka liczba]

> "seven rivers and mountains" in the eighth stanza is an allusion to a stock phrase from Polish folklore, a common opening of fairy tales.

Cat in an Empty Apartment
from the 1993 collection *The End and the Beginning* [Koniec i początek]

Parting with a View
from the 1993 collection *The End and the Beginning* [Koniec i początek]

Love at First Sight
from the 1993 collection *The End and the Beginning* [Koniec i początek]

Negative
First published in *Twórczość* 10 (1996).

. . . too much has happened that was not supposed to happen . . .

We knew the world backwards and forwards . . .
This poem was composed in 1945 and had been slated to appear in 1948 in a collection simply titled "Poems," which was never published. Fifty-two years later, Szymborska chose the poem to open the Polish volume *Selected Poems* [Wiersze wybrane] (Wydawnictwo a5 Kraków, 2000).

Still
from the 1957 collection *Calling Out to Yeti* [Wołanie do Yeti]

A precursor to this poem, "A Transport of Jews" ("Transport Żydów"), was written shortly after World War II.

> "Lech is the name he will have.": Lech is the name of the legendary prehistoric founder of Poland, and is thus the archetypal name for a Polish male.

Starvation Camp at Jasło
from the 1962 collection *Salt* [Sól]

Jasło in southern Poland wasn't itself the site of a starvation camp. The camp was set up in Szebnie, near Jasło, three times during the German occupation of Poland during World War II: from 1941 to 1944 it served at different times as a camp for Russian prisoners of war, and for Polish and Jewish civilians. Different sources have estimated the death toll at anywhere from four thousand to over ten thousand.

Psalm
from the 1976 collection *A Large Number* [Wielka liczba]

Privet is the common name of the ornamental European shrub *Ligustrum vulgare,* now naturalized in the United States and much used in hedges.

The Turn of the Century
Appearing in *Tygodnik Powszechny* in 1983, this was the first poem Szymborska published following the declaration of martial law on December 13, 1981. It later appeared in her 1986 collection *People on the Bridge* [Ludzie na moście].

Children of Our Era
from the 1986 collection *People on the Bridge* [Ludzie na moście]

Torture
from the 1986 collection *People on the Bridge* [Ludzie na moście]

The End and the Beginning
First published in *Tygodnik Powszechny* (January 1992). This is the title poem to the 1993 collection *The End and the Beginning* [Koniec i początek].

Hatred

Originally published in *Gazeta Wyborcza* (June 5, 1992), an editorial decision landed this poem on the front page in a charged political context. The poem later appeared in the 1993 collection *The End and the Beginning* [Koniec i początek].

Reality Demands

from the 1993 collection *The End and the Beginning* [Koniec i początek]

Cannae, an ancient village in Italy, was the setting of the crushing defeat suffered by the Romans at the hand of Hannibal in 216 B.C.

Borodino, a village seventy miles west of Moscow, saw major conflict between the French army under Napoleon and the Russian army under General Kutuzov on September 7, 1812. The battle is chiefly remembered for the heavy casualties suffered on both sides.

Kosovo Polje is infamous for the battle fought on June 5, 1389, between Serbia and the Ottoman Empire that resulted in the collapse of Serbia.

Guernica, a small city in the Basque region of Spain, was subjected to a massive aerial bombing attack by the German air force, aided by Italy and Spain's national Fascist party, on April 26, 1937, at the height of the Spanish Civil War. The resulting massacre is the subject of Pablo Picasso's mural *Guernica* (1937).

Jericho, located on the West Bank of the River Jordan in present-day Israel, was the first Canaanite city to be attacked by the Israelites according to the account given in Joshua 1:1–6:27.

Bilá Hora, near Prague, was the site of the Bohemian defeat at the hands of the Habsburgs on November 8, 1620.

Pearl Harbor, in Hawaii, was a United States naval base attacked without warning by the Japanese air force on December 7, 1941.

Hastings, sixty-two miles southeast of London, is famed as the setting for the victory of Norman invaders led by William the Conqueror over English forces serving King Harold on October 14, 1066.

Chaeronea, an ancient town in central Greece, was the site of the victory of Philip II of Macedon over a confederation of Greek states in

338 B.C. A colossal seated lion marks the grave of the Boeotians who died battling Philip's forces.

Verdun, a garrison town in northeastern France, was reduced to ruins during its historic resistance to German forces in a series of World War I battles that ended in French victory during August 1917.

Actium was the scene of the decisive naval victory of Octavian over Mark Antony and Cleopatra on September 2, 31 B.C. The conflict culminated in the annihilation of Mark Antony's fleet, which was set ablaze.

Hiroshima is the Japanese city on which the United States dropped the first atomic bomb ever used in warfare on August 6, 1945.

Maciejowice is a village near Garwolin, Poland, where on October 10, 1794, Polish forces under Tadeusz Kościuszko were defeated by the Russian army under General Fersen.

Some People
First published in *Tygodnik Powszechny* 34 (1994), recently reprinted in *Selected Poems* [Wiersze wybrane].

. . . *I knock at the door of the rock* . . .

Circus Animals
from the 1952 collection *What We Live For* [Dlatego żyjemy]

Water
from the 1962 collection *Salt* [Sól]

The Ganges, the most sacred river of Hindu India, rises in the Himalayas and flows generally eastward to the Bay of Bengal.

The Nile River originates in central Africa and flows northward to the Mediterranean Sea, forming a delta on the coast of Egypt. At over four thousand miles it is the longest river in the world.

Ys is a legendary Breton town.

Tyre, an important seaport in ancient Phoenicia, sits in present-day Lebanon.

The Caspian Sea, the world's largest inland body of water, is located in southern Eurasia.

The Rudava River, a tributary of the Morava, flows westward through western Slovakia.

Babel: According to Genesis 11:1–9, the Tower of Babel was built by the descendants of Noah who wanted to build it so high that it would reach the heavens. God punished their hubris by confusing their language, so that they could no longer understand each other's speech. From that day onward, the peoples of the globe were scattered, speaking different languages.

Conversation with a Rock
from the 1962 collection *Salt* [Sól]

The terms "omnipotence," "omniscience," and "omnividence" have traditionally been used to describe properties of the Christian God; however, "omnividence" (from the Latin *omnis* [all] and *videre* [to see]) has fallen out of usage and is now archaic.

Birds Returning
from the 1967 collection *Such a Joy* [Sto pociech]

"tissue after tissue bound into a unity / of time and place as in classical drama,": Aristotle in his *Poetics* lays out the rules for a perfect drama, which includes the three unities: time, place, and action.

Seen from Above
from the 1976 collection *A Large Number* [Wielka liczba]

View with a Grain of Sand
from the 1986 collection *People on the Bridge* [Ludzie na moście]

"sky, skyless by nature,": see comments on the semantics of the Polish word for "sky" in the note to "Sky."

Sky

from the 1993 collection *The End and the Beginning* [Koniec i początek]

As in a number of Szymborska's poems (fifteen in the present collection), this poem trades on the two meanings of the Polish word *niebo,* which is used for both "sky" and "heaven." Here Szymborska begins by naturalizing the spiritual or religious, only later to exalt the natural to the preternatural.

"A mole is as high, sky high, / as an owl beating its wings.": the Polish word *wniebowzięty,* is here rendered as "sky high," since it trades more on the word's modern figurative meaning "rapturous, entranced" and contains the root *niebo* (sky). See also notes to the poem "Commemoration."

Clouds

First published in *NaGłos* 17 (1994), recently reprinted in *Selected Poems* [Wiersze wybrane].

In Abundance

First published in *Odra* 3 (1996), recently reprinted in *Selected Poems* [Wiersze wybrane].

"One born under a dark cloud / whose lining gleams for others.": literally "one born under a dark star that shines brightly for others." Szymborska is playing on the idiom "a man from under a dark star," which in Polish means "a shady type." The present translation draws on idioms more familiar to the reader of English.

The Silence of Plants

First published in *Arkusz* 5 (1995), recently reprinted in *Selected Poems* [Wiersze wybrane].

. . . of human kind for now . . .

A Note
from the 1962 collection *Salt* [Sól]

The Cave
from the 1967 collection *Such a Joy* [Sto pociech]

> Pascal: Blaise Pascal (1623–1662) was a French mathematician, scientist, and religious thinker best known for his *Pensées*. Pascal's belief that reason alone could not satisfy human hopes and aspirations became the basis for his defense of religious faith.

A Speech at the Lost and Found
from the 1972 collection *Any Case* [Wszelki wypadek]

> "a singular being of human kind for now,": in Polish the word "kind" denotes both grammatical gender and species, while the combined form "human kind" has a biblical connotation.

A Large Number
title poem to the 1976 collection *A Large Number* [Wielka liczba]

> Dante Alighieri (1265–1321). Italian poet; author of *Divine Comedy*.
> "*Non omnis moriar*" (second stanza): Latin for "I shall not wholly die." (Horace, *Odes,* Book III, Ode XXX, 6). The same quote is found in Szymborska's poem "Autonomy," which is dedicated to the memory of Halina Poświatowska (1935–1967), a gifted Polish poet who died at an early age.

Surplus
from the 1986 collection *People on the Bridge* [Ludzie na moście]

> "local topics fuel a down-to-earth conversation / and people are munching on terra chips.": The Polish word for peanuts is literally "earth nuts." "Terra chips" was substituted to capture this pun. For a

discussion of translation decisions, see Joanna Trzeciak, "In an Abundance of Sudden Wings: On Translating Wislawa Szymborska," *Ruminator Review* 2(54): 20–21, Summer 2000.

On Death, without Exaggeration
from the 1986 collection *People on the Bridge* [Ludzie na moście]

"It can't tell a joke / from a star, from a bridge, / from weaving, from mining, from farming, / from shipbuilding, or baking.": In the original Polish the stanza is constructed on parallels and plays on the double meaning of "to know"—to know how to do something, and an idiomatic expression "to know a joke" meaning to be able to take a joke.

No Title Required
First published in 1988 in *Puls,* under the pen name Stańczykówna. Later included in the 1993 collection *The End and the Beginning* [Koniec i początek].

The Raba River in southern Poland is a tributary of the Vistula (Wisła) River.

"The years of revolutionary anniversaries are rounded off / like stones on the beach.": Szymborska plays on the phrase "round anniversary," literal translation: "what is round are not only the anniversaries of uprisings / but also stones on the shore that one walks around." *Obchodzić* means both "to walk around" and "to celebrate."

One Version of Events
from the 1993 collection *The End and the Beginning* [Koniec i początek]

A Word on Statistics
First published in 1996 in *Twórczość* 10. Reprinted in *Selected Poems* [Wiersze wybrane].

. . . the unthinkable is thinkable . . .

Atlantis

from the 1957 collection *Calling Out to Yeti* [Wołanie do Yeti]

> Atlantis was a legendary island in the Atlantic west of Gibraltar, said by the Greek philosopher Plato to have sunk beneath the sea.
>
> "No, they didn't invent the wheel. / Yes, they did invent the wheel.": this couplet was chosen as a more idiomatic way to render the Polish "No, they didn't invent gunpowder. / Yes, they did invent gunpowder," a play on the saying, "He didn't invent gunpowder," a wisecrack applied to someone lacking in originality or independent thought.

In Heraclitus' River   107

from the 1962 collection *Salt* [Sól]

> Heraclitus was a presocratic Greek philosopher of the sixth century B.C. to whom the saying "You can't put your foot in the same river twice" is attributed.

A Poem in Honor Of

from the 1962 collection *Salt* [Sól]

> "Once, upon a time, invented zero.": Just as in the Polish original, which also plays on the standard opening of fairy tales, "once" becomes the subject of the poem.

Pursuit

from the 1972 collection *Any Case* [Wszelki wypadek]

Interview with a Child

from the 1972 collection *Any Case* [Wszelki wypadek]

> "The handle, the pitcher's ear, will catch any murmur.": In Polish, the handle of a pitcher or a mug is called an ear.

Nothing nothinged itself for me as well
from the 1972 collection *Any Case* [Wszelki wypadek]

> This is an allusion to the infamous proposition *Nichts nichtet* asserted
> by existentialist philosopher Martin Heidegger (1889–1976) in his 1929
> essay "What Is Metaphysics?" *("Was ist Metaphysik?")*.

Under a Certain Little Star
from the 1972 collection *Any Case* [Wszelki wypadek]

The Dream of the Old Tortoise
from the 1976 collection *A Large Number* [Wielka liczba]

> The Emperor: Napoleon Bonaparte (1769–1821), emperor of the
> French (1804–1815)
>
> Jena: A city in southeast Germany, the site of a Napoleonic victory
> over Prussia under Prince Friedrich of Hohenlohe on October 14,
> 1806.
>
> Austerlitz: present-day Slavkov in the Czech Republic, and site of
> Napoleon's victory over the Austro-Russian army under General
> Kutuzov on December 2, 1805.

Pi
from the 1976 collection *A Large Number* [Wielka liczba]

> *"how blithe the throstle sings!"*: From Wordsworth's "The Tables Turned"
> written and published in 1798. In my translation, this quotation has
> been substituted for the line: "My nightingale, fly and sing" from the
> 1841 poem "do B.... z..." ("To B. from ...") by Adam Mickiewicz
> (1778–1855), a Polish Romantic poet.
>
> *"heaven and earth shall pass away,"*: quote from Matthew (24:35).

Miracle Fair
from the 1986 collection *People on the Bridge* [Ludzie na moście]

. . . Oh Muse . . .

Leaving the Cinema
Composed in 1945 and slated to appear in 1948 in a collection titled "Poems," "Leaving the Cinema" was first anthologized in Szymborska's *Selected Poems* [Wiersze wybrane] (Wydawnictwo a5, Kraków, 2000). See note to "We knew the world backwards and forwards . . ."

Rubens' Women
from the 1962 collection *Salt* [Sól]

> Rubens: Peter Paul Rubens (1577–1640) was a Flemish painter, known for his paintings of religious subjects and for his voluptuous female nudes.

Poetry Reading
from the 1962 collection *Salt* [Sól]

> "to be sentenced to the ranks of heavyBlakes": in the original Polish, "heavyBlakes" is "heavyNorwids." Cyprian Norwid (1821–1883) was a great Polish Romantic poet, philosophic in gist.

The Joy of Writing
from the 1967 collection *Such a Joy* [Sto pociech]

Landscape
from the 1967 collection *Such a Joy* [Sto pociech]

> "the sun falls onto a tin pitcher, / and a gaunt man sits at the table / repairing a clock.": may be an allusion to a similar set of images in the poem "Dining Room," the fourth poem in the 1943 cycle "World" by Czeslaw Milosz.

Thomas Mann
from the 1967 collection *Such a Joy* [Sto pociech]

"fins from the Devonian depths,": The Devonian is the fourth period of the Paleozoic era, sometimes called the Age of Fishes.

The original Polish coinage *składanki cacanki* is a hybrid of the Polish word for "jigsaw" and a nonsense word from the lexicon of playground taunts, itself a clipped version of a folk proverb. The phrase "jigsaw marjorie daws" used in this translation, plays on "Seesaw majorie daw" from American playground vernacular.

"it at least permits a certain fish to fly": Flying fish belong to the family Exocoetidae and are characterized by enlarged fins capable of sustaining them in brief, gliding flight over the water.

"a duck-billed platypus": a semiaquatic, egg-laying mammal belonging to the order Monotremata.

Stage Fright
from the 1986 collection *People on the Bridge* [Ludzie na moście]

A Great Man's House
from the 1986 collection *People on the Bridge* [Ludzie na moście]

People on the Bridge
from the 1986 collection *People on the Bridge* [Ludzie na moście]

"people on the bridge": a brocade print titled *Ohashi: Sudden Shower over Atake* by Hiroshige Ando (1797–1858), Japanese woodblock print artist. Szymborska found the inspiration for this poem in a postcard received from a friend visiting London's British Museum, where the lithograph is housed.

Some Like Poetry
from the 1993 collection *The End and the Beginning* [Koniec i początek]

Biographical Note

The younger of two daughters, Wisława Szymborska was born on July 2, 1923, in Kórnik, a small town in central west Poland, to Anna Maria Rottermund and Wincenty Szymborski. She was eight years old when the family moved to Krakow in 1931. From September 1935 until the outbreak of World War II, she attended a prestigious high school for girls in Krakow. Because the school was closed down during the German occupation, she attended underground classes, passing her final exams in the spring of 1941.

Szymborska published her first poem, "I'm Searching for a Word," in a literary supplement to *The Polish Daily (Dziennik Polski)* in March 1945. In 1948, she had hoped to publish a volume titled simply "Poems," but its contents clashed with the Socialist Realist aesthetic that was beginning to take hold. One of her poems, "Sunday at School," sparked a heated discussion in which high school students were prodded to write letters of protest. She was accused of writing poetry that was inaccessible to the masses and too preoccupied with the horrors of war. The volume was never released. A two-year period of poetic silence followed.

Szymborska's book debut came during the heyday of Stalinism. In 1952, she published her first collection of poetry, *What We Live For* [*Dlatego żyjemy*], and was admitted to the Polish Writers' Union and the United Polish Workers Party. Reflecting a youthful enthusiasm for the socialist utopia, both her first volume and its successor, *Questioning Myself* [*Pytania zadawane sobie,* published in 1954], are dominated by politically engaged poetry, with its prescribed anti-Westernism, anti-imperialism, anti-capitalism, and "struggle for peace." Despite the clear propaganda of their content, these poems already distinguished Szymborska among her contemporaries by their adroit elegance. Furthermore, the small number of these early poems that are not overtly political prefigure themes found in her later poetry, namely the playful relationship between the sexes and man's questionable hegemony over nature.

From early 1953, she was editor in chief of the poetry department at *Literary Life* [*Życie Literackie*]. She held high standards for the quality of poetry in the journal, soliciting poems from the premier class of Polish poets. In 1955 the journal published a series of belated debuts by, among others, Miron Białoszewski and Zbigniew Herbert, with commentary by established poets and critics. This run of long-overdue poetic debuts was a bellwether of the coming "thaw," a loosening of restrictions which followed the death of Stalin in 1953 and reached its height in Poland in 1956. Szymborska's 1957 volume, *Calling Out to Yeti* [*Wołanie do Yeti*] is considered one of the important literary events of the Polish thaw. Several poems in that volume, while reflecting Szymborska's reevaluation of her political beliefs, nonetheless transcend their immediate political context. It has been considered a transitional volume, one in which her basic themes begin to take shape. But the collection that marks her arrival as a major poet is *Salt* [*Sól*, l962]. This volume sketches out central themes in Szymborska's poetry. There is the concern with history the uncertainty of love, the place of humanity in the chain of being, the open-endedness of not only the future, but of our distant, little-known past. With this volume, her gift for coaxing the extraordinary, from the ordinary comes to the fore.

In another capacity as columnist at *Życie Literackie,* she was the anonymous coeditor of "Literary Mailroom" from l960 to l968, filling dozens of pages with witty barbs and musings on poetry and its craft, as well as advice for beginning poets. The column was replete with playful rebukes to graphomaniacs, revealing Szymborska's own poetic ideals: precision in diction, respect for the world's diversity and complexity, logical consistency, and attention to rhythm and poetic form.

The late sixties saw several major developments in Szymborska's life. In 1967, when the philosopher Leszek Kolakowski was expelled from the ranks of the Communist party for his "revisionist" views, Szymborska relinquished her own party membership in an act of solidarity. After leaving the party she was prodded to resign as the head of the poetry section at *Życie Literackie* and became a regular contributor of book reviews composed in a form and style distinctly her own: a page-length paragraph written as if in a single breath. From 1990 until the present, her reviews have appeared regularly in Poland's most prominent newspaper, *Gazeta Wyborcza*. Widely appreciated for their whimsy, her book reviews range over a diverse "literary" landscape—from handbooks for handymen to dictionaries of hunter's jargon to catalogs of cactuses to ornithological field guides, with the occasional poetry anthology or translation of Montaigne—a thematic expansiveness rivaling, if not mirroring, that of her poetry.

Over the years, Szymborska has devoted herself to various literary translation projects. Specializing in French poetry, she garnered praise for her translations of Alfred Demusset and Baudelaire as well as fifteenth- and seventeenth-century poets (d'Aubigny, Jodelle, de Magny, Belleau, de Tyard, de Viau, among others). Swimming against the anti-Semitic currents of 1968, Szymborska, who did not know Yiddish, translated several poems by Icyk Menger for an anthology of Jewish poetry. Those same currents delayed its release until 1983.

It was also in the late sixties that Szymborska embarked on another artistic pursuit, this time reserved for her circle of intimates—making collages in the form of postcards to be mailed to friends. Though her favorite hobby grew out of a creative reaction to postal censorship, allowing her playfully to circumvent surveillance by means of images, it continues unabated to this day. Her collages, some of which appear in the present volume, were made in series of say, several dozen, from which she would select one befitting the occasion and the addressee.

For a poet who considers the trash can her most valuable piece of furniture, the seventies were a relatively prolific period. Szymborska published two volumes of poetry, both graced by a strong existential streak. The title poem to the 1972 collection *Any Case* [*Wszelki wypadek*] is a paean to contingency, while *A Large Number* [*Wielka liczba*], which followed in 1976, is bracketed by poems meditating on the immense (as in the title poem) and the infinite (as in the volume's closing poem, "Pi"). Embedded within these magnitudes lie the localized mundane, individuated experiences that provide us the means to grapple with the large. Many of these poems cast a skeptical eye on our assumed primacy over nature and our parochial human perspective, not to mention the failure the grand promise of progress.

Although her sympathies were aroused by the growing political opposition of the seventies, the earlier experience of misplaced trust in the promise of socialism left Szymborska hesitant ever to adopt the role of spokesperson for political causes. Supporter and sympathizer, rather than organizer of initiatives, in 1978 she added her signature to the declaration forming the Society for Scholarly Courses, a type of informal and independent academic society.

With the emergence of the Solidarity movement in 1980, the Society and similar initiatives found themselves briefly freed from earlier encumbrances. Szymborska began her affiliation with the newly formed Krakow journal *Pismo,* whose editorial board included many of her closest friends, among them Kornel Filipowicz, her longtime companion. Following the declaration of martial law on December 13, 1981, the composition of the editorial board and the overall mission of *Pismo* withered as the government imposed demands on it. Similarly, Szymborska's thirty-year association with the journal *Życie Literackie* was abruptly terminated. Under martial law, she chose to publish underground and in the émigré press under the pen name Stańczykówna, a feminized derivation from the name of a sixteenth-century court jester noted for his forthrightness.

Although her poems found their way into a few of the more adventuresome literary periodicals, the political climate prevented her from issuing a volume of poetry until after the end of martial law, marking the longest hiatus between collections. The period preceding the complex transition to democracy saw some loosening of the restrictions imposed under martial law. When it was published, *People on the Bridge* [*Ludzie na moście,* 1986] garnered her praise and several awards, including one from the Ministry of Culture that she declined, and one she accepted from Solidarity. The thoroughgoing naturalism which marked her earlier poetry here extends its domain into the realm of the history of mankind. Clustered in the middle of the collection is a group of poems with an eye trained on history, meditations on the human condition, and the century's lessons still left unlearned.

The poems in the 1998 collection *The End and the Beginning* [*Koniec i początek*] use shifting perspectives to meditate on the fabric of history. Even the most course-altering of events quickly fades from human memory or is reclaimed by organic nature as history and nature stumble forward. This leads not to a nihilism but to an acceptance of human limitation and the significance it bestows on even the most mundane of experiences. *The End and the Beginning* is also in part an elegy to Szymborska's companion of twenty-three years, Kornel Filipowicz, a poet and prose writer who died on February 28, 1990. Throughout these poems there is an awareness that the everyday substance of our social and natural worlds provides both wonder and solace.

Thus far Szymborska has produced nine volumes of poetry: *What We Live For* [*Dlatego żyjemy,* 1952]; *Questioning Oneself* [*Pytania zadawane sobie,* 1954]; *Calling Out to Yeti* [*Wołanie do Yeti,* 1957]; *Salt* [*Sól,* 1962]; *Such a Joy* [*Sto pociech,* 1967]; *Any Case* [*Wszelki wypadek,* 1972]; *A Large Number* [*Wielka liczba,* 1976]; *People on the Bridge* [*Ludzie na moście,* 1986]; and *The End and the Beginning* [*Koniec i początek,* 1993].

Despite critical acclaim and high regard for Szymborska among a large and broad Polish readership, the Communist regime did not shower her with literary prizes. Most of her significant awards came in the eighties and nineties. In 1980 and 1996 she received the Polish Pen Club literary award. In 1991, she was honored with the Goethe Award. An honorary doctorate was conferred on her by the University of Poznań in 1995, and in that same year, she was presented with the Herder Award. The Nobel Prize for Literature was awarded her in 1996.

Except for brief forays into the Tatra Mountains, Szymborska spends most of her time in Krakow, Poland.